PARANOID NATION

THE REAL STORY
OF THE 2008
FIGHT FOR THE PRESIDENCY

★ MATT TOWERY ★

Hill Street Press, Athens, Georgia

A HILL STREET PRESS BOOK

Published in the United States of America by

Hill Street Press llc
191 East Broad Street | Suite 216
Athens, Georgia 30601 USA
www.hillstreetpress.com

Hill Street Press is committed to preserving the written word. Every effort
is made to print books on acid-free paper with a significant amount of
post-consumer recycled content.

Cover design by Bonnie Youngman.
Text design and composition by Jessica Bolfik.

Printed in the United States of America.

Library of Congress Cataloging–in–Publication data on file.
Please contact the publisher.

ISBN 978–1–58818–186–2

★ CONTENTS ★

★

This book is dedicated to the memory of
Rev. James W. Dyer.
A humble servant who never judged, always forgave,
and was always there for those who had no one else to turn to for help.
He was the finest man I have ever known.

PREFACE

I often think of myself as the Forrest Gump of contemporary American politics. I could easily be sitting on that bench, just like Winston Groom's protagonist, telling strangers amazing stories at the bus stop. I have had the pleasure and good fortune of meeting, and in some cases knowing, every American president since Lyndon Johnson. In my most active political years, I knew both Republicans and Democrats at virtually every level of government. From White House chiefs of staff to secretaries of state, I've been blessed in exposure and sometimes even friendships.

One of the most gifted writers of our lifetime is former Reagan speechwriter and current *Wall Street Journal* columnist Peggy Noonan. She has the gifts of clarity, eloquence, and passion in her writing that most of us, rather than envy, simply read and admire. Noonan believes that "history needs data, details, portraits, information, and it needs eyewitnesses." That's where my personal story comes into the larger story of the 2008 election.

As a young kid I was blessed to be bumping around on a regular basis the office of then-Governor Jimmy Carter just as the young and brilliant aides around him were quietly planning a dark horse race for the White House. Years later I chaired Newt Gingrich's political campaigns when Gingrich was Speaker of the U.S. House. My Gump-like experiences range from discussing foreign policy with former President Richard Nixon to spending an evening casually roaming and watching a movie at the White House with Bill Clinton.

In between, I have had the honor—or curse—of running congressional, U.S. senate, and gubernatorial campaigns, campaigns in which I've battled the likes of Democratic strategists James Carville and Paul Begala. And, yes, I've served my time as a Senate aide and consultant in D.C. in the early 1980s. I've known what it is like to be a nominee for high office for a major party in a large state: at age thirty, I was the Republican nominee for lieutenant governor of Georgia. (That also gave me a chance to know what it is like to be run over backwards by a train—Georgia was still very Democratic and I was still very green.) And, unlike a good number of political pollsters and pundits, I have known what it's like to vote as a member of a legislative body, having served as a member of the Georgia legislature.

I write this book as a collector of data and a most fortunate, if accidental, eyewitness to much more history than I could have ever imagined I might see. Just a birthday or two away from age fifty and reaching a transition in my life, I feel it a good time to tie together my nearly four decades of exposure to American political figures, my long study of the contemporary political scene for my nationally syndicated political columns, my years as a political strategist and elected official, and, most recently, my tenure as head of one of the major polling firms to have surveyed the critical caucuses and primaries in the amazing 2008 presidential battle.

Like the fictional character that Tom Hanks brought so vividly to film, I want to sit on the park bench of history and tell how all of the amazing things that I have witnessed from a fascinating, although ultimately concerning, story.

I tell all of this upfront so that you will understand that as I weave this tale of history—the amazing completion of a giant jigsaw puzzle created over decades yet culminating in the greatest political contest of our time, McCain vs. Obama—there is a value to adding personal experiences that, as Noonan mentions, brings stats and punditry to life.

In fact, it is the punditry that best provides an example of a Gump-like moment when, for whatever reason, I seemed to pen something in my national column that appeared not only incapable of being substantiated, but almost fantasy-like in nature. Consider these sentences from my column written for Creators Syndicate in March of 2006. It appeared under my flagship paper, the *Florida Times-Union,* with the headline, "False economy may be based on housing boom." It read in part: "Periodically over the past few years, I've either written about directly or alluded to a potential economic tsunami in the United States. Don't look now, but America's housing market is on the edge of a precipice. More ominous still is that it's not the houses themselves that are a concern. . . . [The] financial foundations may not be able to bear the weight of their debts. . . . My gravest fear is that these high economic times [we are currently enjoying] have been supported by a false economy, one in which people have freely spent borrowed dollars they may not be able to repay without pain."

That was at a time when our economy was booming, and the housing market was ablaze. One might have nominated that column for "Most Paranoid Essay of 2006." Some two and a half years later, it isn't paranoia. It is reality. The stage was set as history collided with reality in the very unusual race for the presidency in 2008.

INTRODUCTION

Early in the campaign it became quite clear that the 2008 race for the presidency would be one for the ages. First, it would be the first truly "open" presidential contest—without an incumbent president or vice president—since 1952. Moreover, the race held high potential to offer up either the first female or the first African American presidential nominee from a major party in U.S. history.

The election itself came in the context of a difficult time in our national history. We had been through almost eight grueling years. Our nation had been attacked. Our economy had dipped and recovered, only to dip again. We witnessed Hurricanes Katrina and Rita, which all but destroyed New Orleans, and then watched helplessly as our federal government fumbled its response to the storms' aftermaths. Filling our gas tank nearly broke the bank; then the banks themselves began to tank. And we've witnessed a war. At first, we supported it. Then even the most unquestioningly patriotic of citizens came to realize that the purpose of the conflict remained unclear.

By the time the 2008 primary season came, the American people didn't know who or what to believe. And that's where the paranoia comes in.

Webster's Dictionary defines paranoia as "a mental disorder characterized by delusions, as of grandeur, or persecution." If that doesn't describe the politics and politicians of the era, nothing does.

And it truly describes the nature of the 2008 presidential contest.

The delusions of grandeur—ranging from national candidates who presumed the presidential nomination would be theirs to elected officials who autocratically moved pieces on the chess board of politics without contemplating that the second-and third-order consequences of their decisions would result in their checkmate—were everywhere.

The sense of persecution—ranging from former Bush foe and unspoken enemy of the "Republican Establishment" John McCain to the first major female candidate for the presidency who went from a target of a vast "right-wing conspiracy" to seeming victim of a rather oblique but omnipresent vast "liberal-wing plan" for her undoing—was the political climate of 2008. (Ironically, the one candidate with the most legitimate claim to being in a persecuted class, Barack Obama, seemed to consistently avoid that claim, but many close to his effort voiced plenty of concerns related to racially motivated conspiracies and attacks.)

And there was plenty of evidence that, beyond the politicians themselves, we as a nation have met *Webster's* definition. We exhibited delusions of grandeur, such as the decision to purchase expensive homes and finance all sorts of debt with virtually no thought of how to make good on the debt. Some were persecuted as they were forcibly searched from head to toe when boarding airplanes, living with the knowledge that somehow, someone was allowed to delve into their personal data in the name of security.

As the presidential primary season developed, certain second—and third—order consequences of seemingly innocuous historical happenings and the insider maneuverings of candidates, political parties, and even the media and pollsters, all came together to create the most amazing presidential election in modern history. The long-ago and little-noticed effort to move one state's primary ahead of others, a single good debate by a preacher-turned-politician, and the results of a major newspaper poll in the most important caucus state that likely influenced the outcome of the primary itself, combined with hundreds of other little-noticed incidents to shape the form of the battle. Suddenly, issues such as religion, devotion to nation, gender, race, age, vulnerability to illness, or issues of personal safety were part of the strange fabric of the 2008 election. Every statement by a candidate, press conference, rally, or visit to a doctor's office only compounded the average voter's concerns. With issues ranging from oil prices and the housing market to the value of fighting wars in the Middle East, everyone was looking over their shoulder, wondering when the next big issue would hit.

And, as usual, many of the same old powers that be—from established political players to the so-called "Media Elite"—would create both suspense and suspicion, along with arguments of collusion and bias. The words "paranoia" or "conspiracy" would turn up, not only in scores of political blogs on the web, but increasingly in mainstream print and broadcast media stories related to the race for the White House. A quick search in Google's news archive section of the word "paranoia" and such names as Clinton, Obama, and Palin alone would, in the closing days of the campaign, yield hundreds of stories from top national newspapers and television news organizations.

As the 2008 political season entered its final months, the nation was twisted into knots over the future of its economy, safety, environment, and role in the world. We had truly become a paranoid nation.

PART ONE

PARANOID PARTICIPANTS

★ 1 ★

EXPLAINING 2008 THROUGH
THE EYES OF HISTORY

When I was barely twenty years old, Newt Gingrich told me
something about politics that would forever remain in my mind.

"It's always about the power," Gingrich said. "Who holds
the power is the only thing that matters in this country."

Newt didn't mean this in a cold-hearted or nefarious way.
Instead, he was teaching a young protégé about the raw and realistic
aspects of the highest level of politics in America. At the time he told
me this, the Republican Party held neither branch of Congress nor
the White House. He knew what it was like to be without the ability to influence policy. And the truth of Newt's maxim can be seen
nowhere better than in the 2008 election.

Would the Clinton family surpass the Kennedys as the
Democratic dynasty for the modern ages?

Would the withering Bush Dynasty be able to keep its imprint
with its candidate, a Mormon former governor of Massachusetts, as
the preserver of control of the party, if not the White House?

1

Would a fast-rising African-American senator be capable of overcoming the widespread if unspoken belief that a black man is electable and would thus bring the party down with him?

Would a man older at nomination than even Ronald Reagan, whose temperament and style had alienated many of his senate colleagues, be capable of overcoming the tattered remnants of the Bush organization? And, moreover, if he did, would that organization quietly allow him to waste away, as they had other GOP nominees, merely to clear the path for some yet unknown reincarnation of their ruling elite in the future?

And would a woman who had been known as Public Enemy Number One to conservative talk show hosts and many conservative voters overcome both a resurrection of the so-called vast right-wing conspiracy and the more unexpected attack from the left wing of her own party?

In 2008 all of the players took place in the fight. And this time, more than at any moment since the would-be Kennedy re-election in the turbulent 1960s, the game was for all the marbles.

It was to be a presidential race about . . . race. Barriers to power for African Americans in America would be pushed to their very limits. Changing attitudes would be seriously tested.

It was also to be a race about war. How deeply should America invest itself in the affairs of nation-states and entities that could cause us great harm, but which have no borders as legitimate enemy nations?

One candidate, a Democrat, had written a bestselling book that propelled him to national prominence, even though he was a relative newcomer to elected office. Youthful and charismatic, optimistic and inspiring, he was suddenly being called one of the greatest orators in a generation. But problematic questions about his religion were being asked, and there was growing concern about some of his associates.

His opponent, the Republican, was older, an outsider even within the true establishment powers of his party. He was an Arizona maverick who spoke his mind freely, often with a degree of bluntness that surprised even his own supporters.

It was all a bit of déjà vu: I'm not describing the 2008 presidential contest, and I'm not talking about Barack Obama and John McCain. Instead, I refer to a dimly remembered race that never was.

Much anticipated, this match-up would have pitted two friends against each other; friends who represented seeming polar opposite views of the direction America should take at a most critical juncture. It was the much anticipated race between President John F. Kennedy, running for re-election in 1964, and his opponent, Arizona Senator Barry Goldwater.

In large part, it was the threat of a Goldwater candidacy—a contest that Kennedy relished—that sent Kennedy to Dallas in November 1963. That and one other thing: a rift within the Texas Democratic Party. Ralph Yarborough, a pro-civil rights U.S. senator, was battling with the more conservative governor of Texas, John Connally. That, too, forced Kennedy to barnstorm Texas that fateful week.

Republicans at the time were split over the concept of a Goldwater bid for the White House. Many within the party's long-standing East Coast leadership establishment viewed Goldwater not just as an extremist, but, more significantly, as a spoiler whose candidacy might set the GOP back for decades in what they feared would be a Kennedy rout.

What would the result have been had Jack Kennedy lived to face Goldwater, a man who was so very different from Kennedy in both style and political philosophy? No one will ever know.

No matter what the results of that contest might have been, the Kennedys could never have an exclusive claim on the title of

America's royal family as long as the potential for two presidents named Clinton existed.

Yes, Bush the elder and his son had actually beaten both the Kennedys and the Clintons to the punch in creating a modern political dynasty. But to the Kennedys and Clintons that really didn't matter. First of all, the Bushes were Republicans. And, to the contrary, George W. Bush's two terms had proven so catastrophic that the term "royalty" would likely never be attached to his family.

Indeed, after the Republicans lost several special congressional races held in the heavily Republican Deep South in the spring of 2008—for seats thought to have been "safe"—top leaders in Congress were declaring Bush's brand of Republicanism so poisonous that it threatened the very existence of the party at every level, even in locations where its hold was considered most solid.

But preserving one's own power within the party has generally been of greater concern than whether one's party's nominee ends up in the White House at the end of any particular election cycle. It's interesting how even seasoned political observers often fail to recognize the fact of political life that battles for a political party's presidential nomination are much more about who will control the machinery than who will win the presidency.

That's not to say that candidates seek the presidency without a myopic concentration on becoming president. But for those in the inner circle of power and money—from lobbyists to those who pride themselves on being big-time fundraisers to the elected and party leaders in each state—it's usually as much about holding on to power within the party as it is defeating the other party in the fall. Preserving or overtaking the "party establishment" has been a longstanding tradition for both Democrats and Republicans.

When one's group of friends doesn't control the party apparatus, one is simply out of the loop. That means that strategists, pollsters, and media experts, vendors who supply everything from direct mail to bumper stickers or sophisticated voter identification and turnout calling, along with a whole cadre of politicians and private citizens who fight to serve on their particular political party's national committee, are no longer of importance. It can mean the loss of significant personal remuneration for the professionals and a loss of prestige and influence for the elected or unelected party activists. To them, this is a really big deal.

That's where we get to John McCain, seemingly despised early on by so many in his party, by everyone except the Republican voters who gave him a string of critical victories in the 2008 race for the nomination. In relatively short order, they rejected all the warmed-over versions of George W. Bush in favor of a maverick, an outsider Republican. To that end, John McCain might as well have been Barry Goldwater in 1964. The comparison was perhaps more a matter of style than philosophy, given that McCain's conservative credentials have proven an endless controversy within segments of his own party.

As for the Democrats, early on it appeared that history would be made much like it was on the issue of religion with Kennedy's election in 1960 but this time on boosting a woman into the Oval Office. But just as John F. Kennedy faced political division within his own party as he headed for Dallas, the Democratic Party of 2008 would find itself embroiled in a deeply divisive battle for power. The history that would be made would be momentous, but not expected. But ironically, the same family, Kennedy, would once again be at the center of the battle for control of their party.

It was, as Newt had taught me years earlier, "all about the power."

★ 2 ★

THE DEMOCRATIC
ESTABLISHMENT AND THE
BEGINNING OF THE IMPLOSION

None of the Republicans' internecine battles that would occur in the 2008 presidential contest compared to the twists and turns the Democratic powerbrokers were facing going into 2008. One thing that most commentators just refused to explain to their readers and listeners—although they knew darn well it was true—was just how much the Al Gores, John Kerrys, and Ted Kennedys of the Democratic Party disliked Bill and Hillary Clinton. There was the most obvious reason: the green-eyed monster. But there were deeper, unspoken reasons as well. For Gore and Kennedy, and to some extent Kerry, there was a sense of political class distinction that existed—even if they themselves did not acknowledge or even recognize it. Both Kennedy and Gore had grown up in the world of Washington, D.C., politics, surrounded by a small cadre of privileged political families, and felt a deep sense of community. That community was never meant to open its doors for a hillbilly from Arkansas and his aggressive, Midwestern wife. That the Clintons became more popular than either Kennedy or Gore was especially galling.

Before the Clintons' arrival on the scene, Kennedy had so disdained that other interloper, Jimmy Carter, that he openly challenged him as an incumbent Democratic president. Carter and his closest friends remain convinced to this day that, had Kennedy not entered the race in 1980 or had he been more energetic in supporting President Carter after he won the nomination, Ronald Reagan would never have defeated Carter.

For his part, Gore would always sting from his own decision not to use Clinton to help secure his election in 2000 as well as the force of Clinton's bitter reaction to that decision. At the time the Gore camp considered Clinton, despite his high approval ratings, a liability in the wake of the Monica Lewinsky episode. Only after the close loss in Florida did it become clear that Clinton appearances in South Florida's African American communities might have increased black voter turnout and won Gore the election.

Going into the 2008 presidential contest, it would be incorrect to say that Senator Hillary Clinton, although considered a likely shoo-in for the nomination, enjoyed the support of the Democratic "D.C. Bubble." The Howard Dean-run Democratic National Committee reflected the Democratic Party's longstanding affinity for a more liberal and Northeastern-based leadership. What the former first lady really enjoyed was their willingness to accept as inevitable the fact that she would win the nomination and wait for an appropriate time to wave the white flag and "join the Clinton team." But then came Barack Obama.

Senator Obama's entry into the contest exposed another of the major hidden points of the 2008 electoral season. I, like so many other commentators, failed to recognize the fact that race, for better or worse, remains one of the most potent and powerful forces in American politics. Going into the 2008 season, I was certain that gender, as embodied by the prospect of our first-ever female presidency, would easily trump race in the Democratic Party, within which her husband was referred to, humorously but sincerely, as "the nation's first black president." I was completely wrong.

Eight years earlier, when researching my book *Powerchicks: How Women Will Dominate America*, I had become convinced that a powerful female candidate would someday emerge, and her gender would not only be an issue but, because more women vote than do men, the issue would work in the candidate's favor.

But in interviewing a wide variety of women in and around politics, ranging from Geraldine Ferraro, the first woman vice presidential nominee for a major party, to a then-rising member of Congress named Nancy Pelosi, one thing was clear. Writer Eleanor Clift summed it up best when she told me that a successful female candidate would not be able to win without embracing her gender as part of her candidacy.

But the Clinton candidacy started out hardly acknowledging the historic nature of electing the nation's first female president. This was unlike the Obama campaign, which made no bones about the fact that, yes, he would be America's first African American president, but so what? And therein was the difference in the approach of the two campaigns that would spell disaster for Clinton.

$\star$ 3 $\star$

SETTING HILLARY'S TRAP:
A TALE OF TWO GOVERNORS
AND A "DEAN"

Born into wealth and privilege, Jeb Bush was once heir-apparent to a new American dynasty—a Republican dynasty to rival the Kennedys. In fact, despite many accomplishments in office as governor of Florida, Jeb remains best known as the Bush who should have made it to the White House—in other words, the "smart" Bush—not the one who, well, you know. A few years ago, I made the mistake of saying something nice about Florida Governor Jeb Bush in a roomful of the state's most powerful lawmakers.

"Don't mention his name," one of them immediately shot back.

I was startled at the reaction, not merely because of the polls showing that Bush was popular with voters, but because everyone in the room, like the governor himself, was a Republican. One of them explained their collective feeling rather bluntly: "He's the most arrogant asshole you will ever meet."

This went on and on. I am not exaggerating in the slightest when I say that the Bush-bashing lasted at least ten minutes. Ironically, the reason I'd been dispatched to Tallahassee was to "speak Republican" on behalf of a client. I doubt these Florida legislative leaders knew of me, but prior to our meeting, they were told of my past roles with Newt's campaign and others, and that long before they had entered politics I had been named as one of the Republican National Legislators of the year (even then that seemed a distant and likely unjustified memory). Clearly they felt that they could vent in front of me, and vent they did.

There's an important lesson here. Even in many states where the governor and legislature are of the same party, styles of leadership can easily lead to sharp divisions within the ranks. I learned that the hard way.

Jeb's big brother W. was careening toward the end of his second term as president of the United States with approval ratings that might kindly be described as dismal. By contrast, Jeb remained at the top of his game through eight years as governor of the nation's fourth most populous state, leaving office with strong polling numbers from the public he served with distinction.

So, believe me when I tell you that in neither demeanor nor philosophy does the Republican governor who succeeded Jeb Bush, Charlie Crist, in any way mirror his predecessor. With a head of silver hair and a permanent tan, Crist looks every bit the part of a Florida governor. But the stereotype ends there. He is a unique public servant, and nowhere is that more evident than in the way he spends money. Or, rather, in the way he doesn't spend it.

"I don't have any debt, and there's a reason," he told a Florida newspaper during his run for governor in 2006. "I just sleep a lot better that way."

Then he added, "It's just how I am."

It's been said that Governor Crist's finances are so simple he could use H&R Block to prepare his tax return, yet you'd never guess that from the sporty cars in which he has always managed to be seen. One of them—a real beauty—happened to be a Jaguar XK8 convertible. Of course, Crist looked so good behind the wheel that few noticed it was an older model, and fewer still had any idea that the successful lawyer had bought the car used.

Like the man said, that's just how he is.

"Charlie Crist eats one meal a day and considers himself generous if he tips a waiter twenty percent," the newspaper article noted. "He uses a single Visa credit card and never carries a balance. He rents a one-bedroom St. Petersburg apartment with a kitchen decor that debuted the same year as *Saturday Night Live*."

The governor may have inherited his appreciation for simplicity from his father, a Greek Cypriot immigrant who was wise enough to shorten the family name from "Christodolous."

Beyond their party affiliation—both are Republicans—the current governor of Florida and his predecessor Bush had very little in common. Bush had been loath to reach out to Democrats. As governor, he was a take-charge leader with little patience for state legislators (of either party) or department heads who failed to see things his way. Crist sought consensus with not only Republican legislators but Democrats as well. In fact, one could hardly find a popular cause or issue that Crist didn't embrace as soon as it emerged.

Immediately upon taking the keys to the Tallahassee state house from Bush at the end of 2006, Crist dismantled Bush-created initiatives and programs, replaced Bush appointees, and pursued an agenda so completely different from Bush's that he received widespread, enthusiastic praise from lawmakers who happen to be Democrats at the same time that he became immediately popular with the selfsame Republican legislators who had battled his predecessor.

"That across-the-aisle lovefest couldn't be further removed from the proudly partisan crusade of Crist's predecessor, who fought hard against many of those initiatives," noted an article in *Time*.

Yet, the two governors did team up on one thing—and it just happened to be the thing that would eventually turn the 2008 presidential primary season into the most riveting and emotional set of contests in the modern era. The fact that their motive was completely different is beside the point.

Before he left office Bush, a brilliant political strategist if nothing else, extracted a promise from the promising young incoming speaker of the Florida House of Representatives, Marco Rubio, who—unlike many of his colleagues—liked Bush immensely. It was a promise easily made and easily kept. Rubio pledged to move the date of Florida's primary election ahead of the South Carolina primary, leaving only the Iowa and New Hampshire primaries and the relatively small Nevada caucus ahead of Florida.

The intention, of course, was to posit Florida as the new American microcosm, the very first point of entry for both Democrats and Republicans in the 2008 election cycle. Or so the polls had hoped. The result would prove to be another thing altogether!

Even before talk of moving the Florida primary first began—well over a year before the actual legislation that made the move possible was passed in 2007—there was no joy in the inner circle of the Howard Dean-led Democratic National Committee. Dean, privately no fan of the Clintons, was distressed over the seemingly inevitable Hillary Clinton nomination. With Florida's heavily senior and longstanding pro-Bill Clinton vote, Dean knew that no Democratic candidate had any hope of stealing this critical piece of the nomination puzzle away from Hillary Clinton. That is, if the Florida primary were to count.

When talk of moving the primary started to get serious, Dean and his Northeastern cronies dug in their heels. They had no intention of allowing the Florida primary to be moved to January, eclipsing the importance of and focus on the Iowa caucus and the New Hampshire primary, not to mention cutting in line ahead of the South Carolina primary. That would give Clinton an early and likely insurmountable lead. Even to allow the fourth most populous state to vote prior to Super Tuesday in early February would likely still assure Clinton a momentum-shifting Florida victory as she headed into February.

Dean's position was clear: The rules of the DNC would be upheld, and any state holding a primary prior to South Carolina's should be penalized by having its delegates' votes go uncounted in the race for the nomination. This hard-line stance was firmly supported by Dean's fellow New Englanders, who wanted to maintain their newly recovered control of the national Democratic Party.

The Florida Democratic Party, although controlled by factions friendly to Clinton, was usually bankrolled by a powerful cadre of Democratic trial lawyers. Their candidate of choice, one-time attorney John Edwards, was likely to fare better if the fallout from an advanced Florida primary move left Clinton and her supporters high and dry.

Nearly a year before the contest in Florida, Dean met with a prominent group of trial lawyers in West Palm Beach. As he made his pitch for their financial support for the party, only one of the big-dollar donors raised the issue of Florida's delegation being penalized because of a move made by a Republican-controlled legislature. As one of these politically active donors put it, "[The national Democratic Party] didn't know if it would kill off Clinton, but they knew at the very least it gave their man a better chance, and that was fine with them."

But with Clinton leading in virtually every poll of every major early contest a year out, Florida seemed to the Clinton camp like something not worth fighting over. And so, in silence, the Clinton campaign watched as Iowa moved its caucus to January 3, New Hampshire followed five days later, and South Carolina moved its primary up to January 26, three days ahead of the contest in Florida.

Suddenly the DNC ban on seating Florida's 210 delegates seemed much more important to the Clinton campaign. When Michigan moved its primary to January 15, Democratic leaders punished the state by stripping it of all 156 of its delegates to the national convention the following year. The danger to the Clinton campaign became clear.

In the end, it was the perfect set-up for the destruction of the Hillary Clinton candidacy. Was it a conspiracy to deprive Bill and Hillary Clinton of the creation of America's greatest Democratic political dynasty? There were certainly some longtime powers in the Democratic establishment, particularly in the Clinton camp, who were starting to think so.

In the middle of May 2007, about the same time that the Republican-controlled Florida legislature was moving toward making the state's primary the preeminent contest of 2008, I quietly observed Hillary Clinton at one of her countless high-dollar fundraisers, mixing with a crowd of seventy-five or so. The senator was relaxed, smiling, clearly feeling no pressure. It was a warm and sunny day.

After more than forty-five minutes of casual conversation with old friends and new admirers, she went to the front of the large and well-appointed family room of her hosts' spacious house to address the assembled. Senator Clinton led with an affable joke about the Clintons' longtime confidante, powerbroker Vernon Jordan, who stood quietly in the corner of the room.

"I've known Vernon for over forty years. I was in kindergarten, and he was a young lawyer," she quipped.

There was little or no talk of Barack Obama. There was perhaps a reference to experience, but most of Clinton's brief talk was targeted at reversing the "damage" to the nation that had been imposed by the Bush administration. She noted that George Bush wasn't a conservative, but rather "a radical ideologue." Clinton almost seemed to be saying to her upscale, corporate crowd that being a little conservative isn't bad, it's being a radical that's the problem.

But Clinton wasn't exactly reaching for the mantle of the conservative for herself. Universal health care, a concept that sends shivers down the spines of most conservative voters, was the senator's number one campaign issue.

Her continued devotion to the very same idea that had caused such heartburn for her husband's administration and had ensured the success of the Republican Revolution of 1994 notwith-standing, the Senator Clinton of 2008 was very different in look and demeanor from the First Lady Clinton I first observed in the 1990s.

It was a hot day in the April of 1994, and the first lady was buzzing around the East Room of the White House, clearly not happy as she played hostess to a reception honoring the U.S. athletes from the successful Winter Olympics held that year. As luck would have it, I took a seat in a row close to the podium, next to the last open aisle seat. When a clearly irritated Hillary Clinton chose to sit next to me while she talked—make that complained—to staff over the tardiness of both the president and vice president, I felt even more ill at ease.

As the minutes dragged by, she chided the staff over the president's habitual tardiness. She couldn't get a good answer as to why he was so late and demanded to know why Gore was equally behind schedule. By the time her husband arrived, she was close to furious.

The president clearly recognized that he was in hot water. He immediately thanked his wife for trying to keep "cool" in an increasingly hot room while he tried to make it out of the Oval Office. It was hot alright, but the heat he felt was Hillary Clinton on low boil. To give her credit, the first lady didn't like keeping Olym-pic medalists and other guests waiting for nearly an hour while the president likely dillydallied, as he was known to do.

Years had passed, and now it was her own schedule and her events that mattered. Her political and personal maturity was obvi-ous simply by comparing her demeanor in those White House years to her role as a U.S. Senator and leading presidential candidate.

Something that Hillary Clinton said at the posh fundraiser in 2007 proved truly ironic just a year later. In response to an audi-ence member's question about her husband and his political success she said, "I've always said Bill Clinton is the luckiest man I've ever known." True enough—at the time. But even the luckiest of people someday meet a challenge they can't overcome. For Bill and Hillary Clinton, that obstacle was the timing of the Florida primary and its far-reaching consequences.

★ 4 ★

BARACK OBAMA:
THE <u>REALLY</u> NEW
NEW NEW THING

In 1999, a few years after the Internet had become commonplace, the digerati took to a book called The *New New Thing*. I recalled Michael Lewis's portentous title when a youngish, African American first-term senator named Barack Obama entered the race for president several years later. Obama grew to national prominence as "The New New Thing" on the political scene, not because of his ties to Washington, D.C., or even his home state of Illinois, but through his ties to the region that had given rise to the revolutionary technology and Web-based successes of the late 1990s and early 2000s, Silicon Valley. Truly, Obama is "The Really New New New Thing."

In the spring of 2007 a young man Chris Hughes joined the Obama campaign. To even the most astute political observer, that would mean little. If the basic facts of his biography were known—that Hughes was in his mid-twenties and a graduate of Philips Academy and Harvard University—one would likely draw the conclusion that he was a fairly typical first-time campaign staff worker.

Well, first-time campaign worker would be correct. But Hughes was far from a typical young staffer. With his Harvard roommates, he co-founded Facebook, one of the hottest social networking websites, in 2004. As Obama's coordinator of online organizing, Hughes went to work applying the very same community-building skills that he and his partners had developed to make Facebook a hugely successful and growing entity.

In a February 2008 story in SiliconValley.com, Steve Westly, a former eBay executive and California co-chair for Obama, stated that the tech-savvy campaign supporters had "put together the very best online fundraising tools." It's entirely appropriate to refer to a website branded SiliconValley.com in a discussion about Obama. It is a real explanation for how the Obama campaign took an attractive but little-known candidate and catapulted him into political super-stardom, because Obama's ascent is best chronicled from the virtual world of Silicon Valley than from the old world of Capitol Hill.

In the same story, the online publication reports that, "the Obama campaign has gone beyond fundraising in its use of its new technologies. The goal is to foster a community that does more than give money—writing e-mails and letters to superdelegates, attending house parties and other events, making phone calls and going door to door." Friends of Obama on Facebook received automatic news feeds from the campaign, mass-text news updates on their phones, and reminders of where to vote in upcoming primaries.

In fact, Obama campaign intimates would later reveal that the Facebook-style communities it developed branched out in every direction and kept on growing and likely helped crown Obama the King of Caucuses. A caucus often attracts fewer participants than a primary. The Obama campaign had a very motivated and organized community of participants. Through their intricate internet-based organizations, the Obama campaign was able to marshal troops in greater numbers than the other candidates.

Much about Barack Obama remained unknown to most of the voting public. His youth spent outside the United States, his years at Harvard, and his meteoric rise as a political figure in Chicago remained hazy for even the majority of his supporters throughout his fight for the nomination.

But two things were clear early on. Obama was a fresh and mesmerizing voice in a field of known political entities. And more importantly, while the Clinton campaign was raising money the only way presidential candidates had ever known—high-dollar meet and greets—Obama's organization of twenty-something computer nerds were building a completely new Democratic party—and funding it through online donations five and ten dollars at a time.

★ 5 ★

THE O FACTOR:
OR OOPS, THERE GOES
THE OPPOSITION—
KERPLOP!

I first realized Hillary Clinton might be vulnerable in the Democratic primary when I saw early reports that a handful of major
Hollywood moguls had broken ranks with this liberal, apparent
shoo-in, a woman who as both first lady and senator had rubbed as
many elbows in Tinseltown as in Washington.

Hollywood is made up of people who, by and large, have an
almost childlike understanding of politics and the way things really
work, not just in Washington, but also in every other corner of the
nation. Yet for various reasons ranging from its ability to raise money
to its ability to confer celebrity by association on a candidate, this
entertainment capital has exerted a major influence over presidential politics for many decades.

Frank Sinatra, whose popularity as a singer and actor was
at a peak during John F. Kennedy's 1960 campaign, became one of
the first major Hollywood stars to use his public appeal in order to
actively support a presidential candidate. The race became one of
the first in which "modern" political ads were crafted and used for
television. It certainly was the first in which a major celebrity played
a role in such ads.

Sinatra not only campaigned and raised funds for Kennedy, he even went so far as to record a version of his 1959 hit "High Hopes" with new lyrics to Jimmy Van Heusen's tune touting the handsome, idealistic young Democrat.

Everyone is voting for Jack
'Cause he's got what all the rest lack
Everyone wants to back-Jack
Jack is on the right track.
'Cause he's got high hopes
He's got high hopes
Nineteen-sixty's the year for his high hopes.
Come on and vote for Kennedy
Vote for Kennedy
And we'll come out on top!
Oops, there goes the opposition—ker—
Oops, there goes the opposition—ker—
Oops, there goes the opposition—KERPLOP!

Kennedy was fighting for the "new generation" of Americans to whom Sinatra was an icon. In a race as incredibly close as the Kennedy-Nixon contest, one can hardly undervalue the importance of having the active support of someone as popular as Ol' Blue Eyes in one's corner.

As president, Lyndon Johnson never enjoyed the youthful attributes of JFK, but he certainly understood the power that Hollywood held in influencing the public.

Superagent and studio head Lew Wasserman, for many years the single most powerful man in Hollywood, made sure that he took advantage of the new Hollywood-Washington connection with his support of Lyndon Johnson. And he got a lot in return. It was at Wasserman's urging that Johnson appointed close adviser Jack Valenti to head the newly emerging Motion Picture Association lobby. Valenti soon turned the MPA into one of the most powerful organizations in the world of politics and helped Wasserman's television production company, MCA, sustain laws that prohibited TV networks from producing their own entertainment programming. That incredibly unfair law survived well into the 1990s.

In 2000, Meg Ryan and her soon-to-be-ex-husband Dennis Quaid, along with Nora Ephron and others, visited the White House for a screening of their film *Hanging Up*. Don't ask me how or why, but my wife and I were also invited. It's part of the Forrest Gump quality of my life that I wrote about in my preface. There I was, laughing and joking with Bill Clinton but finding the scene a bit surreal, like the scene in which the Tom Hanks character appears in footage with Lyndon Johnson in *Forrest Gump*.

After we watched the movie, President Clinton took about twenty of us, made up almost entirely of the Hollywood crowd, on a long, roaming tour of the White House. Clinton knew the history of every room in a degree of detail that shocked me. I had never known a major political leader who took the time to learn such detail about paintings and furniture while in the heat of political battle.

I note this story, however, more for the reactions on the faces of the celebrities—those of us who were mere mortals were icons—seeing the White House in such a private and revealing manner. The looks on their faces were the equivalent of the look on my face when I walked the Warner Brothers lot one day with a friend and actually entered the house (actually a façade attached to rather ratty unused rooms) of my hero Clark Griswold (played by Chevy Chase) from *Christmas Vacation*. To my Hollywood companions, the Oval Office was obviously as daunting as a Hollywood set would be to someone used to the world of politics.

Of course, some entertainers end up becoming politicians. But not all of them end up becoming president, like Ronald Reagan. More often you end up with Ben "Cooter" Jones of The *Dukes of Hazzard*, Fred "Gopher" Grandy of *Love Boat*, or Jesse "The Body"

Ventura, who, as a professional wrestler, clearly did more acting than the rest of them combined.

And then there was Sonny Bono, who rode the Republican Revolution created by Newt Gingrich and served as a Congressman from California from 1995 until his tragic death in 1998. Bono was a very kind and amiable man who was as much in awe of where he was and what he was doing as our officials in Washington were of his past entertainment stardom.

Ironically, it was Bono who first spotted the star treatment Newt was receiving when he became Speaker of the House. Bono warned Newt that the experience of suddenly finding oneself on every magazine cover and television program could, as had been the case when he and his former wife Cher became international stars, cause one to lose perspective.

It must have come as quite a shock to the Clintons—Hollywood's darlings during Bill's two terms in office—to discover their cachet going the way of Norma Desmond's career in *Sunset Boulevard*.

In early 2007, invitations went out to seven hundred Democratic donors and activists to meet Barack Obama at a February reception in Beverly Hills. Each was asked to contribute $2,300, the maximum annual amount federal law allows. Hosting the event were none other than Steven Spielberg, David Geffen, and Jeffrey Katzenberg, three of the most influential moguls in show business.

An article in the *Washington Post* mentioned the event rather ominously as the potential decline of the Clintons' longstanding power in Hollywood. While pointing out that Hillary Clinton continued to enjoy widespread support among such stalwarts as actress Elizabeth Taylor, former Paramount Studios chief Sherry Lansing, and magnate Ron Burkle, the article went on to note growing celebrity support for her upstart opponent.

"A parade of celebrities have expressed support for Obama," the article continued, "including Oscar winners George Clooney and Halle Berry and TV talk show host Oprah Winfrey."

One can easily imagine Hillary's heart sinking as she read that last name. If not, it should have.

Oprah is, after all, much more than just a talk show host. The mere mention of a book on her nationally syndicated talk show will make an author's career. *O, The Oprah Magazine* claims an average monthly readership of 2.7 million. In polls of the most admired women in America, Oprah Winfrey ranks right up there with Hillary Clinton. Oprah's decision to throw her weight behind Obama represented the biggest impact that perhaps any other entertainment celebrity has had on a presidential campaign. Ever.

Before Oprah's decision to actively campaign for Obama in the early primary state of South Carolina, the longstanding relationship between major black leaders and the Clintons seemed to be holding up well, and my polling firm showed Clinton carrying nearly forty-five percent of the vote among African Americans who intended to vote in the state's Democratic primary.

That came to a crashing halt one Sunday in December 2007, when Oprah appeared in the eighty-thousand-seat Williams-Brice Stadium in Columbia, South Carolina, alongside the Illinois senator she believes can save the world—or at least do a better job of not destroying it.

"There are those who say it is not his time, that he should wait his turn," Winfrey told the capacity crowd. "Think of where you'd be in your life if you waited."

The dean of South Carolina political writers is Lee Bandy, who after years as the top political newspaper reporter in the state, covered the race for the presidency in 2008 for our company. He attended the rally and called me afterward.

"You won't believe it," he enthused. "I've never seen any kind of political turnout for an event like that, ever. They were even tailgating, like it was a major sporting event."

Lee described the scene in greater detail. Yes, he said, there were many African Americans in the crowd, but there were also many whites, particularly young whites.

Our polling firm had the distinction of having been the first pollsters to record the "O" Factor on the Democratic primary battle. The results were astounding, as we very quickly discovered. The percentage of black support for Obama had risen from forty-five percent before the rally to over seventy percent immediately afterward. Clearly, black voters had determined that they had a genuinely viable African American candidate seeking the White House. Not a Jesse Jackson or an Al Sharpton. An actual, for real, go-the-distance contender.

Since then, I have thought more than once of an endorsement made nearly fifty years ago by the father of Martin Luther King Jr. The senior King, known as "Daddy King," had been a lifelong Republican, but he switched his support from the Republicans to John F. Kennedy in 1960 after the candidate's family helped secure MLK's release from an Atlanta prison after his arrest at a protest.

Daddy King's move inspired a mass exodus of black Republicans to the Democratic Party and helped Kennedy enormously among black voters. But Oprah Winfrey's public endorsement in the 2008 election, proved, I believe, to move more votes and have a greater impact than any other ever provided by an African American leader or celebrity.

In another Gump-like moment, I was involved in sponsoring a charity event that Oprah Winfrey was kind enough to attend. I joined five or six people in a reception area where we waited to greet Winfrey before she was to speak to the assembled group. I was the only male in the group and the only one who wasn't famous or important.

When she entered the room you could feel her charisma. I mean really feel that presence. And I did something I've not been known to do. I moved back and away from her and her friends, barely having the courage to step forward to shake her hand. Talk about politicians being overwhelmed by entertainers! I was completely taken aback by Oprah Winfrey.

Later that day I sat directly behind her on the dais as she delivered a powerful message about her own youth. Her inspirational speech was spellbinding, and I knew I was witnessing something the likes of which I would never see again. What was really weird was that the spotlight aimed at her as she spoke created—I'm not joking—a halo effect around her as I looked at her from my seat.

So it came as no wonder to me that when Oprah Winfrey took the stage in South Carolina she brought it home for Barack Obama.

Hillary Clinton was now facing the most potent force imaginable—the African American woman of our lifetime. Things were going to get rough. And Oprah's was not the only iconic name the Clintons would be forced to confront.

★ 6 ★

BARACK OBAMA AND
THE KENNEDY CONNECTION

James J. Unger died unexpectedly in April of 2008. To most Americans, his was a name that would have no meaning whatsoever. But in Washington, D.C., and indeed around the nation among many of America's top professors, political leaders, journalists, and attorneys, Jim Unger was a legend.

A slight man with a forever youngish look, Unger was known for his three-piece suits, his bow tie, and his walking cane (carrying on it the carved head of a duck, a self-deprecating tip of the hat to his own "duck-like" appearance). Unger was a mentor or friend to many of the brightest minds in America.

He was best known for his years as the debate coach at Georgetown University in the 1970s and 1980s (later establishing himself at American University). Jim Unger was a known staple in the intellectual community of Washington, D.C. For the most part, ties to Sen. Edward M. Kennedy heavily dominated that community.

Among close Kennedy associates who had worked with or known Unger were fellow world-class former college debaters such as nationally renowned Professor of Constitutional Law at Harvard Laurence "Larry" Tribe and longtime political consultant (and author of Kennedy's famed 1980 Democratic convention speech) Bob Shrum.

I had been recruited by Unger to attend and debate for Georgetown. I was accepted by the University in 1978, but before the first day of the school year started, Unger announced that he was taking an unexpected sabbatical, and within two days my bags were packed, and I was headed back home.

But during the time I was being "recruited," I became intensely aware of the fact that Unger was part of the "glue" that helped bind the Shrums and Tribes of the Kennedy world. And here I was, a child from the land of Jimmy Carter.

The word of Ted Kennedy's seizure and subsequent revelation of a serious and malignant brain tumor ironically came at the end of the same week that Hamilton Jordan, who ran the Carter reelection battle against Kennedy, finally succumbed to a rare form of cancer. Of even greater irony, Ham's first bout with cancer had come years earlier in the form of a brain tumor. He defeated the first tumor and went on to describe his victory in a bestselling book, *No Such Thing as a Bad Day.*

But in 1980 it took all that Hamilton and the rest of the Carter team could muster to stave off a Kennedy effort to take the presidency away from Carter. The attempt started off badly but seemed to gain momentum as it went along. Shrum's speech, delivered brilliantly by Kennedy, is widely regarded as one of the top political speeches of modern times.

In doing my research, an early maximum donation and endorsement by Larry Tribe in March of 2007 caught my eye. While the Kennedy family remained neutral in the race, Professor Tribe taught Barack Obama at Harvard Law. Obama was a research assistant for Tribe. I felt it unlikely that Larry Tribe would be pushing the candidacy of a young man whom he had stated "was the most impressive all around student" that he had ever taught if he felt that by doing so, his efforts would be severely contrary to the desires of Senator Kennedy. By the way, there's nothing wrong with that—it's called loyalty.

And to be fair, Tribe is of such prominence in the legal and academic communities that he could easily have made the political decision on his own, likely realizing that his move would open Kennedy's eyes to Obama as a serious alternative to Hillary Clinton.

Tribe had moved on the political chessboard in the past, seemingly apart from Kennedy, but more likely in concert. In the 1980 presidential campaign, while research shows references to Tribe providing legal advice to the Kennedy campaign, Tribe's more public involvement was in assisting Congressman John Anderson—who had run unsuccessfully as a "liberal" Republican in the primary season—gain access to the ballot as an Independent candidate in the general election.

The move, reported by *Time*, was perhaps part of a plan created by Tribe and his longtime friend Shrum to use Anderson as a bargaining chip—with hopes that Anderson would remove himself from contention if Democrats at their convention dumped Jimmy Carter in favor of Kennedy.

Whatever the plan, if there was one, it never worked. And as for the press picking up on Tribe's close association with Kennedy (which became crystal clear when Tribe led the charge for Kennedy against Supreme Court nominee Robert Bork), well, the *Time* article didn't even spell Tribe's first name correctly.

Often the Kennedys developed enduring relationships that the working press failed to notice. Consider the case of Sen. Obama.

After word of Sen. Kennedy's first illness became public, Obama himself began to shed greater light on the depth of the relationship with Kennedy. And after just a few phone calls, I confirmed that Kennedy had played a key role as a mentor to Obama long before he was sworn into office.

To put it bluntly, I would have been shocked if most of the Kennedy inner circle were not encouraging and, at the very least hoping, for Obama to emerge as the upset kid. Consider the description of Obama that Ted Kennedy provided in a story that ran in the *Washington Post* in July 2006: "There is enormous thirst within the Democratic Party, within the country, to have new directions, new solutions, new ideas."

But in that same article, Kennedy said that he did not know Obama well enough to counsel him on whether to run for president in 2008. With all deference to Kennedy, that simply was not the case.

Shrum stated publicly that he had first become aware of Obama as a rising star through Tribe. And a *New York Magazine* article published in June 2008 clarifies the situation. The article suggested that Kennedy wanted to remain neutral going into the primaries, in part because of the presence in the race of Sen. Joe Biden and Sen. Christopher Dodd, both close friends of Kennedy. Nevertheless, "Ted had been one of the first to encourage Obama to run; he thought the moment demanded a candidate who could inspire the nation."

The article summed up what went unspoken throughout the primary season but that was obvious to Clinton supporters in hindsight. It states, "There was another reason for Ted Kennedy to carefully weigh his decision. The debate wasn't just about who the best Democratic candidate would be, or who had the best chance to beat the Republicans. It was also about which candidate would best perpetuate the Kennedy political legacy."

But when neither Biden nor Dodd emerged as a "John Kerry of 2008" dark horse, the debut of Barack Obama that was to set the stage for a candidate for the future suddenly transformed into an immediate choice that met Kennedy's criteria.

Consider Kennedy's words in endorsing Obama on January 28, 2008. He described Obama as a candidate who "can lift our spirits and make us believe again." Kennedy praised Obama for providing change and new solutions. In essence, it was the very same thing he said in the interview of 2006.

A quick look at the words of another key Kennedy elder, Ethel, finds her introducing Obama during the summer of 2007 as "the next president of the United States." It would be early into the 2008 season when she would endorse Obama officially, noting how much his passion for the poor and disadvantaged reminded her of her own late husband, Bobby Kennedy.

Not all Kennedy family members ended up supporting Sen. Obama as the 2008 season grew increasingly tough. Robert Kennedy Jr., and his sister Kathleen Kennedy Townsend both declared support for Hillary Clinton. But in the business of politics, particularly when it is a family business as it is with the Kennedys, hedging bets and covering all bases is just as traditional a practice as it has been among prominent Republicans.

More directly, the Kennedy family relationship with the Clintons in prior years, while less strained than that with the Carters, was nevertheless always one formed with caution and restraint. There is little doubt that Clinton was enamored with the Kennedy family, even when he and Hillary set sail one day with Clinton as the president and Ted Kennedy as merely a senior senator and the "skipper."

Still, a repeat Clinton in the White House meant that history books would likely recall a more powerful "Royal family" in the Democratic Party than the Kennedys.

Even on paper, and long before it came to fruition, a run by Barack Obama in the 2008 field, from a purely strategic standpoint, could possibly enhance the chances for, say, a Joe Biden or Christopher Dodd (one of Kennedy's closest friends)—both more regionally and personally comfortable for the Kennedys as a Democratic nominee than would be Obama.

From the outset, strategically speaking, Obama, even if he failed to catch on with white voters, could certainly hold on until

South Carolina and Super Tuesday—both opportunities for the rising star to, at the least, take away the otherwise automatic Clinton vote in the African American community.

At least that's how many around the Clintons viewed the Obama campaign in its early stages. The Clintons weren't so naïve as to not pick up on Bob Shrum's comments on *Meet the Press* over a year before the race, in which the then little-known Obama candidacy was touted as having real potential.

It's fair to say that, as it was in 1960 when JFK sought the presidency, in politics all things remain, as they say, local. Given that, the Clintons faced a near impossible uphill battle against the Kennedys in 2008. Former Massachusetts Democratic Party chairman and a close confidante of Senator Kennedy, Philip Johnston, who first met Ted Kennedy in Bobby Kennedy's 1968 campaign for the presidency, signed on with Obama in March of 2007.

David Axelrod, Obama's chief strategist and political general in both his race for the Senate in 2004 and the 2008 campaign, had spent plenty of time getting to know the Kennedy forces as he guided another groundbreaking African American candidate to a historic win as the first black governor of Massachusetts.

Stories began to circulate that Ted Kennedy was actually "pushed to the breaking point" when, during an appearance in New Hampshire, Hillary Clinton failed to correct the words of another speaker who spoke before her. The previous speaker had suggested that Lyndon Johnson was responsible for the Civil Rights Act, a statement that is fighting words to the Kennedys, who know that President Kennedy had announced his support of the legislation on national television prior to his assassination.

But no one would ever convince close Clinton supporters, much less one as wise to the world of real politics as the Clintons, that a simple failure to correct history could lead to a ringing endorsement of Obama by the most important names in the Kennedy family.

It made perfect sense that, when word spread that not only Ted but also JFK's eldest and only remaining child, Caroline, would both endorse Obama, the Clintons flew into a rage—one perhaps more justified on Hillary's part than anyone else's.

When Sen. Kennedy was pushing for the newly elected President Clinton to appoint his sister Jean Kennedy Smith to the position of Ambassador to Ireland, it was, according to Kennedy biographer Adam Clymer, Hillary Clinton who made the calls around D.C. to find out just how much the appointment meant to Kennedy.

Hillary convinced Bill Clinton to name Smith even as Bill likely demurred. Few knew that Clinton had endured ridicule at the 1992 Democratic National Convention in Atlanta from Kennedy insiders when his big moment in the spotlight as a lead speaker turned into an unending snore-athon that nearly ended his career.

And why would the Kennedys have cared? Because slated to speak at that same convention was the late John F. Kennedy Jr., in his political debut to the nation. There could be only one "shining star" besides the nominee (Governor Mike Dukakis, who had a hard time shining), and it had to be a Kennedy.

Indeed it was. Clinton, still the "Hillbilly Kennedy wannabe" in the eyes of some, felt the sting.

But Hillary was far more pragmatic. And within no time flat she provided the Kennedys what they wanted.

The Clintons didn't hesitate. They reminded Ted Kennedy how they had backed a female Kennedy for a tough post—one in which she was later formally reprimanded by the U.S. State Department for having allegedly punished staffers who had opposed her efforts to give a visa to the head of the controversial Sinn Féin, Gerry Adams, in the mid 1990s.

The Clintons' fear that the Kennedys would attempt to block a Clinton "dynasty" was coming true.

And many Clinton supporters felt that the message was made crystal clear when Barack Obama announced that Caroline Kennedy would become part of a three-person (soon depleted to a two-person, after the resignation of one of the members) committee to conduct a search for Barack Obama's vice presidential nominee. At the time of the announcement, one top Clinton friend said, "It's like posting a 'Need Not Apply' sign in the window as far as Hillary is concerned. They (the Clintons) won't grovel."

As it turned out, the Clinton associate was correct. The committee never even requested any information that might be necessary to consider Clinton. Her name was never in consideration. When asked about Hillary Clinton, Caroline Kennedy demurred by noting how important it was that she continue leading in the Senate.

The sadness of Ted Kennedy's illness quickly replaced the bitterness of the 2008 race for most Democrats. In fact, the 2008 nomination of Barack Obama might have been the greatest and most obvious statement of the power the Kennedy family continued to wield within the Democratic party.

But for the Clintons it had become fairly obvious, as it had to the Carters who preceded them, that the power and might of the Democratic party's own version of a "Northeastern Establishment," one dominated by the Kennedy family some forty-five years since the death of President Kennedy, could still prove a force to be reckoned with.

★ 7 ★

THE REPUBLICAN ESTABLISHMENT
AND THE SEEDS OF ITS UNDOING

Politicians often care more about who ends up controlling the party than who wins the election. Just as the fight between Clinton and Obama in 2008 was a battle for control of the Democratic Party, the battle for the GOP nomination was simultaneously with a battle for control of the Republican Party.

That battle for the heart and soul of the GOP really began in the late 1950s and early 1960s. For all practical purposes, the modern Republican Party really came into existence when Dwight Eisenhower agreed to run for president and finally brought an end to the domination of the GOP by the so-called Taft Wing of the party. However, it was the Rockefeller family, the descendants of the once-richest man in America, John D. Rockefeller, who really got things moving in those years.

Long a source of immense wealth and power behind the scenes of American politics, some of the Rockefellers suddenly became willing to get their hands dirty. Key family members were allowed to run for and hold public office. And, without a doubt, the emergence of Nelson Rockefeller as governor of New York in 1959 was the single most important cog in the public side of this wing of the Republican Party.

The early seeds of the rise of the Rockefeller Republicans are chronicled in Richard Nixon's memoir. Nixon bemoaned the fact that he had agreed, as vice president, to take the lead in the GOP's effort to gain seats in Congress in the midterm elections of 1958. "The defeat [for GOP candidates] was massive," Nixon wrote. "The next morning I heard that one of the TV commentators told viewers that the big winner of 1958 was Nelson Rockefeller, who had been elected governor of New York by a wide margin—and the big loser was Richard Nixon."

Ironically, two diametrically opposed wings of the Republican party converged in an (ultimately unsuccessful) effort to deprive Nixon of the 1968 GOP nomination. Even as Nixon appeared to have the nomination sewn up going into the party's national convention in Miami Beach, he was struggling with the rich folk. "I was trying to keep power out of the hands of Nelson Rockefeller. He was far from giving up [an effort to win the nomination]," Nixon recalled in his memoir. "He continued his frantic polling up to the eve of the convention and arrived in Miami Beach with armloads of statistics."

Nixon recounted that Ronald Reagan entered the convention as a potential candidate and that "the marriage of convenience between Rockefeller and Reagan was now operating in full force. Rockefeller worked on the Northern and Midwestern states while Reagan tried to branch my Southern flank."

Nixon's comments are more telling than one might guess. Lacking the Ivy League credentials and moneyed background of Rockefeller, Nixon always viewed himself as an outsider within his party. He constantly engaged in a dance with the Rockefeller wing of the GOP in order to simultaneously placate and keep in check the powerful organization. I learned this after returning to the states in 1983 while studying for an advanced degree in International Relations at Cambridge University. During my break in studies I met, of all people, Richard Nixon. I had already endured my first stints as a staffer in a major campaign and in the office of a U.S. senator and had read and heard enough to know of Nixon's disdain for Ivy Leaguers and "party hacks."

The then-former president was more than kind. And he had not lost his political skills. "You know, most Americans know about Oxford, but Cambridge is where the really smart guys go." Clearly, with my southern accent and unsophisticated style, he could tell I was not likely to know a Rockefeller Republican, much less a Rockefeller. And Nixon, just beginning his emergence from his so-called exile after resigning the presidency in 1974, had not lost his ability to politic.

Ironically, the one time Richard Nixon reached out to the Rockefeller family allowed them to gain a foothold in Republican politics. After his 1968 victory, President Nixon felt emboldened enough to seek their advice as to the best possible adviser on foreign affairs. They suggested Henry Kissinger.

Kissinger had worked with politically active members of the Rockefeller family since the early 1960s, and whether valid or not, more than one political observer has given almost total credit for his subsequent success to that family of wealthy string-pullers.

Let me address one of the most widely disseminated but rarely contradicted conspiracy theories out there. It involves the Rockefeller family, other powerful individuals, and organizations such as the Trilateral Commission, the Council on Foreign Relations, and the Bilderberg Society. Such discussions can be found as early as 1972 in Professor Thomas Dye's *Who Is Running America?*, in which Dye improbably states that, "Kissinger's rise to power depended more upon his affiliation with Nelson Rockefeller, the Rockefeller Foundation, and the Council on Foreign Relations than his intellectual achievements."

Generally speaking, once these organizational names appear in any book, either the author is banished to the realm of the nutjob, or the existence and importance of such organizations is completely dismissed. But Dye built a reputation for being one of the nation's foremost academic experts on the topics of leadership in society and government.

Dye's work was completely academic in nature. Others have taken such research and attributed far more sinister motives and actions to such institutions. While I think it unwise to dismiss a writer merely for suggesting that these institutions might be significant players in party politics, I'll be so bold as to say it's equally unwise to consider a less conspiratorial view of their existence. They are more than relevant, both on the Republican and Democratic sides of the political equation.

I'm not saying the "Internet activists" have the whole thing right. They don't. But what they're saying isn't as far out there as you may think.

In the 1970s, various ultra-conservative organizations, such as the then-popular John Birch Society, began to shift their focus from matters of race to what they believed to be the United Nation's effort to create a New World Order. They perceived the U.N. to be profoundly anti-American in nature, a confederation of global manipulators. Chief among the subjects of the ultra-conservatives' ire was the Trilateral Commission.

Efforts by the Birchers to suggest a nefarious secret society composed of a small handful of elites working together to thwart the will of the people was actually given a small boost every time it was mentioned simply because it almost always got the same reaction. Opinion leaders in government and the media denied the existence of the organization.

But the Trilateral Commission did indeed exist, in some ways for the very reasons put forth by the extremists who wished to expose it as some sort of stealth government. The Trilateral Commission was established in 1973 by David Rockefeller, the financial leader of the Rockefeller family, along with assistance from members of other organizations, such as the Council on Foreign Relations. The stated goal of the commission was to bring leaders of multinational corporations and certain elected and appointed leaders from the United States, Western Europe, and Japan to meet periodically to provide coordination and steering guidance on issues of importance to the various nations.

In the 1970s, this was a relatively novel concept, and the existence of the Trilateral Commission added fuel to the fire for those who viewed the world as increasingly becoming controlled by a so-called elite.

The Rockefeller family's involvement in such organizations as the Trilateral Commission only fueled the suspicions, particularly among the Republican party's broader base of support, that there truly were two factions of the GOP—the so-called Rockefeller Republicans and the conservative wing of the party. Among those who held disdain for the commission was Ronald Reagan, whose mid-to-late 1970s commentaries, carried in syndication on radio stations, jabbed indirectly at a power elite and often took aim at institutions such as the United Nations. Ironically, Richard Nixon, who gave Kissinger entry into the party, was disdainful of the so-called Rockefeller Establishment. Yet it seemed that Nixon, despite his feelings of resentment over powerful dynasties such as those of the Rockefellers and the Kennedys, not only enjoyed flirting politically with their powerful friends, but almost enjoyed his obsession over what they were "really up to."

It was Richard Nixon's paranoia over the whole Kennedy family, and by the early 1970s specifically Senator Edward Kennedy, that resulted in much of the political mischief that led to the Watergate scandal and Nixon's ultimate resignation. The uncovering of this political scandal proved that conspiracies do exist. It also demonstrated how the power of the press could thrust a public event into the center of our lives.

★ 8 ★

JESUS AND THE FAT MAN:
HOW THE REPUBLICAN ESTABLISHMENT
WAS TAKEN DOWN IN A SINGLE NIGHT

Going into the primary season of 2008, the Republicans were overcome with malaise. John McCain was obsessed with the troop surge in Iraq and had a string of recently mishandled bills, such as the much-maligned "immigration compromise." While every other campaign was gearing up in the summer of 2007, McCain was cutting back as fundraising lagged and staff costs became too high. Actor-turned-senator-turned-actor-again Fred Thompson entered the race late and with all the energy of a snail. Republicans seemed moribund and, under the dark shadow of the strong national dislike for George W. Bush, uninspiring.

Through much of the year leading up to the Iowa Caucus, former New York Mayor Rudy Giuliani led the Republicans in national horse race polls. Even more so than on television, Giuliani was charismatic in person, and he remained one of the more spontaneous and lively of the candidates.

My first inkling that America's Mayor might not be ready for a presidential run came when I learned in January 2007 that a nearly two-hundred-page campaign plan, which included a very detailed list of all of the candidate's weaknesses and vulnerabilities, was either lost or stolen from the Giuliani campaign while the candidate and his aides were traveling.

While it is true that all campaigns develop campaign plans, Giuliani's went overboard. Usually, issues such as the personal vulnerabilities of a candidate, if they are actually committed to paper, are circulated in very discreet memos among a very tight circle of loyalists. The naïveté of the Giuliani campaign plan revealed that the frontrunner was using some awfully old and outmoded tools in setting up his campaign. And to lose the thing was just plain sloppy.

The candidate who was thought to be the savior of the "sane conservative" crowd was former *Law and Order* cast member Senator Fred Thompson. Thompson entered the race late in the summer of 2007. I was plugged in to what Thompson was up to because of my professional and personal relationship with his entertainment attorney, Joel Katz, and because of the fact that my longtime mentor, former U.S. Senator Mack Mattingly, was a core member of the Draft Fred effort.

So on a hot day in July 2007, Joel, Mack, and I were on hand as Thompson launched his first major "exploratory" fundraiser at the home of his national campaign finance chair. Thompson had just returned from a vacation but seemed exhausted. Our company's polling of his potential entry into the race suggested that, in many states, he would take an immediate lead or be close to the top of the candidates.

But Thompson's first speech was a bomb. The former senator rambled from one topic to another and seemed to lack any of the so-called fire in the belly that he would need to make it through the week, much less an entire presidential campaign.

It would prove to be a challenge to watch the man most believed to be a very capable Republican leader as he reached— time and time again through the caucus season—deep within, trying to find that fire.

Mitt Romney owned that so-called GOP establishment. I knew it the moment I was invited to interview the former Massachusetts governor as he was "considering a possible exploratory committee" in 2006. I arrived for the interview with one of my business partners who had spent years on the Republican National Committee and in elected office. Before we even entered the room at a private club, I could tell from the people who greeted us—all figures in both Bush 41's and Bush 43's organizations—that Romney would be the candidate of choice of the so-called GOP Establishment in 2008.

From the start you could tell that this guy was bright, chose his words carefully, and fit the mold of a GOP nominee. But that was the problem. From the monogram on the shirt to the tasteful cufflinks to the Ultrabrite smile, Romney seemed, at least to me, too polished and pre-packaged for a guy who claimed he hadn't really made up his mind about an exploratory committee. The interview was focused almost entirely on the success Romney had enjoyed in his home state in reforming health care.

I left the meeting thinking, "Well, here we go again—this is their candidate." He's not bad, but I didn't see him connecting with the everyday voter. Team Romney wasn't all that thrilled when my column based on the interview stated that the Republican "in-crowd" was attracted to Romney because they felt comfortable with him. Like President Bush, Romney has a long Republican pedigree. (His father, George, was chairman of American Motors Corporation from 1954 to 1962 before serving as governor of Michigan from 1963 to 1969 and was a candidate for president in 1968.)

But trust me, I know these people, and Romney is their kind of guy. And they desperately wanted someone like them. Alternatively, they are terrified of anyone who is too independent in his thinking, someone like, for example, John McCain.

Don't get me wrong. I had and have no problem with Romney's ideology insofar as it matched up with traditional GOP ideology over the past two decades. After I left that interview with Romney, I rode the elevator with a close friend who had served as a former Republican National Committee member, and we both marveled that Romney was undergoing the same set-up to run that Bush 43 had enjoyed, and it was even being staged by basically the same people.

Mitt Romney's bid for the GOP nomination did not end in early 2008 on the snowy battlefields of Iowa or New Hampshire, as is widely assumed. The same is true for Rudy Giuliani. Without realizing it, both these formidable players had been out of the game months earlier, when their candidacies collided with the Internet Age.

The turning point was November 28, 2007, the night of the CNN/YouTube debate in St. Petersburg, Florida. Romney and Giuliani might as well have been Alexander Litvinenko, the former Russian spy who ate radioactive sushi. When something like that happens, you don't know it right away, but it's all over. You have become the walking dead.

This showdown in the Sunshine State—or, more accurately, in cyberspace—took place after all the candidates from both parties had already debated in the tried-and-true format on the major television networks. For the CNN/YouTube debates, however, thousands of questions were uploaded by average citizens, and it was up to the network's political unit to select a relatively small number of questions to fill up a debate that would run for just a few hours.

The Democrats' version of the CNN/YouTube format, broadcast from South Carolina on July 23, 2007, had been a huge success. It embraced technology, it was inclusive, and, while some of the questions were less than impressive, it was anything but boring. The homemade video inquiries kept the whole thing lively and far removed from the paint-drying dullness of a standard debate.

The Democratic candidates rolled with the punches, answering most of the questions with a mixture of humor and venom in addition to the usual dodging and ducking.

But one question chilled the blood of Republican operatives watching the debate, men and woman already assumed to have ice water flowing in their veins. In the question, a Claymation-style snowman with a high-pitched voice asked about the issue of global warming. Republicans found two things off-putting about the question. For one thing, the question was about global warming, an issue on which GOP candidates had yet to find a satisfactory, comfortable position. For another, the style of the question just wasn't . . . well . . . dignified. The humorous nature of the animated character caused the minds of these angst-ridden Republican strategists to run wild. Immediately, they realized just how painful it could be for their strait-laced—and relatively boring—candidates to be forced to answer questions from a faux snowman. Did any of the GOP candidates have the sense of humor to take such a question?

Moreover, with their innate fear of the perceived liberal agenda of CNN, could they trust the network not to sabotage one or all with a similar attack question, without even a human face that could be identified as the culprit? It is, after all, one thing to look Anderson Cooper in the eye and deliver some kind of reproach, as the senior President Bush had done in his famous confrontation with Dan Rather while running for president in 1988. But if he were taking questions from Gumby and Pokey, not even Ronald Reagan could get away with saying, "There you go again!"

The GOP's immediate, virtually unanimous reaction was to denounce the debate as undignified and to refuse to participate in their own already-scheduled YouTube-style contest. Mitt Romney, looking very presidential at the time, was perhaps most leery of the setting and format.

Romney posted his concerns about the YouTube-style debate on—where else?—YouTube. That drew a response, almost predictably, from the animated snowman himself. Romney caved. And, one by one, the other Republican contestants relented.

Eventually, all the GOP candidates would be on board what they feared could be their Titanic.

As it turns out, Romney had plenty to worry about. But it wasn't the questions, or some cartoon character delivering the questions, that would prove to be his problem. Mike Huckabee, former governor of Arkansas, was folksy, witty, likeable, and, until the debate, had been almost completely ignored. As a minister, he no doubt would appreciate being called David to Romney's Goliath. And it's a fitting analogy. Goliath fell that night.

The modern Mahaffey Theater in St. Petersburg was the perfect setting for the cyber debate. While many Americans may think of the city as God's waiting room, in truth, the shuffle board courts are long gone. This is a trendy and dynamic sister city to the more commercial and staid Tampa, which sits just across the bay.

Just hours before the debate, members of the working media were deluged with copies of a story broken by Politico, a relatively new and very influential player in niche political publishing, disclosing that frontrunner candidate Rudolph Giuliani had spent a king's ransom in taxpayer money on security while courting his lover and soon-to-be wife, Judith Nathan. To many in the pressroom, especially reporters for the *New York Post* and its ilk, the report simply added detail to what they already knew. The disclosure could prove politically challenging should Giuliani actually get the GOP nomination.

The timing of this story revved up not only Giuliani's camp, but Romney's as well. Blood was in the water, and a shark from Massachusetts was circling.

When the debate began, both men were on pins and needles and, in no time flat, were viciously attacking one another, almost to the exclusion of the other candidates. Slowly, John McCain and Fred Thompson entered the fray, with McCain giving a relatively good, if low-key performance, and Thompson at least demonstrating that he had not quietly expired while everyone else was arguing.

But it was Mike Huckabee whose sunny disposition on an otherwise dark and daunting stage shined through.

Our polling firm and others had already shown Huckabee's popularity starting to build, and not just in Iowa, but in Florida as well. But regardless of these little blips on the radar, no one—and I mean no one—thought Huckabee was anywhere close to being a contender prior to the debate.

After the debate was over, it was an entirely different matter. Why?

Huckabee's light and genial manner fit the YouTube debate style so well. After Romney and Giuliani fought bitterly over inside-baseball questions about immigration, the questions moved to other issues. Huckabee, the former Baptist pastor, was asked in one of the video questions "what would Jesus do" on the use of the death penalty.

Huckabee's response not only got him out of a tight jam, but also won him both the debate and the momentum needed to head into Iowa as the grassroots favorite. "Jesus was too smart to ever run for public office, Anderson," Huckabee told Anderson Cooper. "That's what Jesus would do."

The debate over, reporters moved to a traditional "spin room," located just steps away from the press area. There, various spin doctors were assigned to represent the various candidates and present to the traditional television networks their drastically differing takes on what had just happened.

It is illegal to poll by telephone in any state in the union after 9:00 PM, so broadcast and cable networks make sure that their contests end after that hour. That ensures that viewers will have to listen to hours of their own analysts and the various campaigns declaring who won the debate and why. Consequently, TV viewers are usually stuck listening to the same old pundits, experts, and armchair quarterbacks attempting to analyze the debate and declare the winner of the contest.

Sometimes, Frank Luntz—a longtime pollster, focus group guru, and GOP strategist—will appear with a focus group of undecided viewers who use hand-held devices that measure their reactions at various moments in a debate. Frank does good work, and it's actually very accurate, as well as entertaining. But his approach doesn't tell you, based on a statistically valid sample, who really won the debate.

Teaming up with the Florida Chamber of Commerce, our company came up with a very innovative way of polling Floridians immediately after the debate.

We knew we could not call viewers. We knew all along that the debate would end well after the 9:00 PM cutoff on the East Coast. Instead, some ten days before the debate, we took the unprecedented step of randomly calling over one hundred thousand registered Republicans in Florida to ask if they were going to watch the debate, if they were undecided as to who they would vote for, and if they were willing to call a toll-free number after the debate to register who, in their opinion, had won the debate. Just to cover our bets, we also planned a massive telephone survey in Iowa, where, legally, we still had a 10-minute or so window of time to call as the debate broadcast was wrapping up. Both polls worked.

We qualified the necessary number of random Florida respondents who met all of our criteria, including being undecided as to candidate preference, and enough of them phoned in to give the survey a statically valid margin of error. Huckabee won the Insider Advantage/Florida Chamber of Commerce poll with a whopping forty-eight percent of respondents. Rudy Giuliani was a very distant second, with only eighteen percent saying he'd won. Even more telling figures came out of Iowa: Our poll showed that out of 1,035 Iowa Republicans who were registered to vote, the results were again overwhelmingly for Huckabee. So we knew very quickly, for a fact, what everyone else had only sensed.

The spin room was a battlefield littered with crushed egos. Young people stood alone holding signs for each devastated little camp. So just imagine the pride of the kid holding up the Huckabee sign as the entire herd of reporters rushed straight at him.

Just before I could reach Governor Huckabee to tell him he had won the debate, a really large gentleman entered into an argument with a Huckabee aide and shoved the young man to the ground, an odd occurrence in a secure spin room. I finally did tell Huckabee the results, which seemed to surprise him a bit.

That night the fat man who smacked Huckabee's aide to the floor wasn't the only one with a knockout punch.

Establishment frontrunners Giuliani and Romney had been taken down in a single night as well.

★ 9 ★

AND THEN THERE WAS RON . . .

There were others in the GOP contest. U.S. Representative Ron Paul was the most colorful and had the most passionate supporters. His level of support was dismissed by most political pundits, and his message, some of which was based on surveys of Republican voters, was obscured by the dismissive nature of the coverage of his race.

Paul has had a long love-hate relationship with the Republican Party. In his initial term in Congress, he was the first member to support term limits, then a position unpopular among Republicans. He ran as the Libertarian nominee for president in 1988. After he criticized the first two years of the Gingrich-led House for failing to curb spending and implement other legislation that he had supported, Newt and the GOP actively supported a Democrat who switched parties to run as a Republican against Paul in his 1996 Republican primary election. The move backfired, and Paul was reelected to Congress. Paul became, for some, the candidate for those who felt most fervently that the GOP had sold out on its principles.

Paul and his supporters wanted a drastic decrease in government intervention in their lives. They feared the globalization of the U.S. economy and the instability of the nation's monetary policy. In many ways their positions mirrored most closely those of Ronald Reagan in 1980.

But party activists were quick to say that the rather rumpled and disheveled Paul was in no way like Reagan and refuted the idea that he shared much in common with Reagan's philosophy. Having really been around during that time period, I thought their argument was not completely compelling. In fact, listening to Paul in several debates, I wondered whether Reagan himself, the Ronald Reagan of 1980, if alive, would not have voted for Paul. One must remember that the Ronald Reagan of the late 1970s and 1980 spoke far more bluntly than did Reagan the president.

Of course, in polite Washington society, suggesting such an idea was simply unacceptable. When I wrote these thoughts in my nationally syndicated newspaper column, I had a huge response from Paul supporters. Over time I noticed that even members of the Reagan family were saying that Paul was not a true Reagan-type candidate. Perhaps not, and they would know best. Nevertheless, Paul's support and influence grew much larger than most political leaders and opinion-makers could have imagined.

One of the most underreported stories of the 2008 race was that of the percentages that Paul, a man written off by insiders from the start, actually received in some of the caucuses and primaries. For example, in Iowa Paul was within three percent of John McCain and outdistanced Rudy Giuliani by a full six percentage points. In New Hampshire he was virtually tied with Giuliani and Huckabee and led Fred Thompson. Romney captured an overwhelming fifty-one percent in the Nevada caucus (which followed those in New Hampshire and Michigan), but Paul came in second place with fourteen percent support, ahead of all others—including McCain.

It wasn't until the Florida Primary that Paul finally leveled off at the three percent he would receive in many other contests before momentum clearly moved towards McCain.

What many in the media missed was the critical question: Had Ron Paul not been in the race, where would his core constituency have gone? Would his voters have pushed a remaining conservative on the ballot, say Fred Thompson, into a more competitive range in Iowa? Or would they have given the somewhat unconventional Mike Huckabee their support in South Carolina, thus edging McCain out?

Written off as a flake by the press, Paul's impact on the race and the passion of his supporters were never truly recognized. The question—a source of great paranoia for the GOP going into November—of where Paul's votes will go in the general election remained.

With former Republican Congressman and better-known Libertarian Bob Barr now in the race, the unnoticed percentages for Ron Paul could loom large in tight battles in swing states in the fall. Party officials were concerned that there existed in 2008 a certain percentage of reliably Republican voters who, for whatever reason, would have a hard time warming up to the GOP nominee. Whether these individuals might simply sit out the election or cast their vote for the Libertarian candidate remained a mystery. In fact, it was difficult for anyone to quantify any of this.

But the day in July of 2008 that Ron Paul announced his Rally for the Republic, a campaign event to be held in the same location and on the same date as the 2008 Republican National Convention, he sold over 6,000 tickets. Given that the GOP convention was expected to attract, according to news reports, 45,000 attendees, Paul's gathering seemed insignificant. But in reality, fewer than 5,000 delegates and alternates would be allowed to occupy the floor of the Republican convention.

With his unique mixture of scheduled speakers, including former Minnesota Governor Jesse Ventura and Barry Goldwater Jr., Paul's gathering would technically have more actual active participants than the Republican convention. His effort would be to fill the 15,000-seat

Target Center in Minneapolis. As one Republican mused, "Maybe we ought to increase the delegate and alternate numbers down the road!" Ultimately Paul's "Rally" would attract nearly 15,000 attendees, but virtually no attention from major national broadcast or print media. The event, held in the other "Twin City," Minneapolis, was to those watching political coverage that week, a non-existent event. The question would remain, would Paul's small but devoted base play the same role it had played in the early caucuses and primaries—this time not to the unintentional benefit of John McCain, but rather to a thin but critically important detriment.

★ 10 ★

BOB BARR AND OTHER
CLOSE ENCOUNTERS
OF THE THIRD KIND

On Memorial Day weekend of 2008, Bill Clinton's onetime nemesis won what some might consider the booby prize of American politics—the Libertarian Party's nomination for president.

While some may remember Bob Barr as the hard-charging Republican Georgia representative who fired the first legislative volley in the impeachment of Bill Clinton, he is hardly a household name outside of D.C. and his home state. But the impact Barr might have on the 2008 presidential race was not lost on the McCain camp, or at the very least, not on those within his campaign who had any horse sense.

As George Will wrote in a cogent *Newsweek* commentary, the mustachioed and curly haired Barr's personality "is an acquired taste." It's a taste I acquired back in the mid-1980s.

After I had left the staff of U.S. Senator Mack Mattingly, there arose an opening in the office of U.S. Attorney for the Northern District of Georgia. At that time, Bob was a new face on the scene in Cobb County (the same county that would become Newt Gingrich's home base when he was Speaker of the U.S. House of Representatives), then the center of the GOP in Georgia. Mattingly was urged from all sides to appoint a Cobb attorney, and Bob's background at the CIA and his Georgetown Law School training combined to make him a good fit.

If Bob's public persona seems cold and dour in 2008, it's fair to say that his private one was about the same in the 1980s. Although not everyone involved in the selection process was thrilled about Barr's appointment to succeed the brilliant and later-to-become Bush's number-two man in the Department of Justice, Larry Thompson, they certainly weren't embarrassed either.

No sooner did Bob get into his position than he started an aggressive corruption case against one of only two GOP House members in Georgia at that time, Pat Swindall. (Whether Swindall did anything wrong or not I could never really discern, but of course the charges that stuck, as is commonly the case, were related to perjury.) Media coverage of the case made Bob well known in Georgia. Soon he set his sights on Congress. The problem was that he wasn't a welcome participant among the Georgia Republican establishment.

In 1994, as Newt was spearheading the GOP takeover of the House, word spread that he was quietly supporting Barr's opponent in a Republican primary for a potentially winnable congressional seat in November.

Gingrich, who was publicly neutral, saw a quick fix. He asked the two political names then most closely associated with him—Mack Mattingly and me—to be co-chairs of Barr's campaign. We were not enthusiastic about the job because we were involved in helping candidates in much bigger races, but we did at least attach our names and some nominal effort to Bob's race. Bob won rather handily and, I might add, almost completely through his own efforts.

It would be fair to say that Newt's attitude towards the new Congressman entering under his new speakership was at best ambivalent. In fact, several times I requested Bob to help us out with the sharing of staff or in matters more political in nature. Each time he would request that I find some invitation to some senior House GOP meeting or some other (and I thought reasonable) display of Newt's recognition that they shared neighboring districts. Barr wanted Gingrich's attention.

This becomes all the more interesting when one considers the role that both Gingrich and Barr would later play in the Clinton impeachment controversy. Let it be known that when Bob first decided to take on Clinton, he did so without much encouragement from Gingrich or many of the top House leadership. The impeachment was, for quite some time, "The Bob Barr Show."

It was only when trusted Gingrich ally and House Judiciary Chairman Henry Hyde began taking an interest in the matter and new revelations came forth that the whole impeachment concept began to grow legs. Bob had finally received Newt's full attention—like it or not.

I was opposed to the Clinton impeachment effort for very strategic and pragmatic reasons. I wasn't condoning anything he did, but I knew that the sort of indiscretions he was accused of occurred all over Washington, and that the GOP was going to look like the biggest bunch of hypocrites in the world. And in conducting numerous focus groups around the country, I learned first-hand that women in particular did not like the way the GOP lawmakers appeared to be turning what they considered a private matter into a high crime and misdemeanor. Clinton's approval ratings stayed high, and the Republicans just dug themselves a hole.

I appeared on Chris Matthews's *Hardball* program right in the middle of the decision by the House to launch an official inquiry into the impeachment of Clinton. I was there to promote my book *Powerchicks*, but as I was the chairman of Newt Gingrich's political campaign organization, Matthews shot rapid-fire questions at me about the impeachment, an impeachment that held no interest for me. (Anyone who knows how quick Matthews is probably knows that I didn't get much book promoting done that night!)

After Barr and his legal posse failed to convict Clinton in a Senate trial, the Georgia legislature, still dominated by Democrats, tore his district into twenty pieces and forced him to run against another D.C. fixture, Congressman John Linder. Our firm polled the race for a local affiliate, and the results showed Barr getting creamed. Barr did indeed lose and was banished into a world that he disliked immensely, a world outside the spotlight.

Years later, our company had the opportunity to occupy a particularly well-appointed suite of offices. Although I felt the space was too expensive, we took it anyway. About the same time, I ran into Bob at a restaurant, where he mentioned that he was looking for upscale space for his strategic consulting firm. And although our businesses had nothing to do with each other, we divided up the space and, for several years, his staff and mine coexisted peacefully.

Obviously, when he and I were both in the suite at the same time, which wasn't that often, we would sit and talk about the issues of the day. During those years I came to know a far more humorous and self-effacing Bob Barr than I had known in previous years. Bob is a smart man who actually has a very middle-of-the-road view on life, even if his deeply held passions, gun rights and privacy rights among them, belie that fact.

Over a year before his announcement, Bob and I discussed the possibility of his making a run for the Libertarian nomination. At the time he was not very enthusiastic but thought it was an intriguing idea. As a guy whose job is analyzing political polling data and observing the inner workings of politics, my talking to Bob about running as a Libertarian for president was the equivalent of a plastic surgeon casually mentioning to a friend, "Hey, you could really make that nose look great with a little work!"

In the spring of 2008, Bob called to tell me that he was relatively sure that he would indeed pursue the Libertarian nomination. I had to admit that I felt he could likely outperform past Libertarian candidates, given the Ron Paul factor and his credentials as a one-time mainstream Republican.

Bob and I still have a friendly relationship. After all, I'm probably the only one who would burst into his office and call him Mr. Personality just to hear that sly little chuckle that lies beneath his otherwise stern façade.

There was, of course, one by-product of a Barr candidacy that, although not his purpose in running, was nevertheless inescapable. If Bob were to catch a political wave, he had the potential to shear three or four points off of the Republican nominee's total and tilt tight swing states towards Barack Obama.

As Bob secured the votes of the eclectic collection of delegates to the Libertarian convention, I was asked by several reporters what impact I thought Barr's entry into the presidential race would have. I had yet to be convinced that, absent a large war chest, Bob could do much more than generate a lot more free media coverage than any past Libertarian nominee and would be lucky to garner two or three percent of the national vote. Then again, two or three percent for a third-party candidate could make a huge difference, as Florida proved in the 2000 cycle with the candidacy of Ralph Nader.

I felt that Barr's greatest chance to pose problems for McCain could be found in those southern states where the African American vote is high and there is a highly energized white Democratic vote. There were also some other, smaller western states where a well-run Libertarian candidate could make waves. That combination held the potential to undo McCain if he were to lose a few percentage points to Barr or a Ron Paul-type alternative party candidate.

Our firm, InsiderAdvantage, conducted a poll in Georgia around the time of Barr's nomination that showed him taking McCain to under fifty percent in this, one of the big ten electoral states. Barr is a Georgian, of course, but the poll was still significant. It meant the state could, at least hypothetically, be up for grabs once the huge proportion of black voters was taken into account. The same could be said for some other Southern states, such as Virginia,

Alabama, and North Carolina, but only if Barr could raise money and that was a big "if."

Was this a bad thing? Well, not if you were a Democrat who wanted an Obama victory. But even for those Deep South Republicans, those publicly pressured to curse Barr, there was a silver lining.

In recent elections, most of the South, absent Florida, has become a virtual given for GOP victory. As a result, the elected officials and Republican activists in those states are less important, as are their views. If one knew one had their vote, then why pay much attention to their views? Just cash their checks. Really, all they had to offer was money—always gladly taken. But with the Libertarian nominee guaranteed access to the ballot in all of these states, Bob Barr—Mr. National Rifle Association—forced the Republican nominee to concentrate on the region, addressing its issues and embracing its party leaders. And that was not limited to the South. Numerous states that had gone Republican in a string of presidential election cycles were being contested by Barack Obama, thus opening the door for Barr to attempt to chip away votes as well.

Barr's biggest problem would prove to be, as I noted, money. And that leads me to one of the best kept secrets I've ever known.

I am no stranger to third-party candidates for president. First some background. I recall the man I met as a young child and for whom I served as personal page, the flamboyant former Georgia Governor Lester Maddox. Maddox was known as one of the South's last segregationists, although Lester never really "got it." He insisted his stand on integration in the South in the 1960s was an issue of "states' rights." Later he waged a largely ignored presidential run as the American Independent Party's candidate against, of all people, his successor to the governor's office, Jimmy Carter, in 1976.

Zell Miller would later rise to become Georgia's most successful governor of the modern era. He brought the state its successful lottery, which funds the HOPE scholarship awarded to any student who meets certain academic requirements in high school. The nationally known Miller had served as Governor Maddox's chief of staff. I was too young to understand the hoopla over Maddox, and Zell spent all of his time trying to keep Maddox out of trouble with the media, an impossible task.

I had known Miller since I was a young man. His political career had taken him from state legislator to a moderate lieutenant governor of Georgia to a left-of-center candidate in the 1980 Democratic primary against Herman Talmadge (the man my candidate, Mack Mattingly, went on to defeat) to a victorious progressive governor and later as an appointed and then re-elected U.S. senator who had turned conservative. Few of the politicians I have known or studied could match the skills of Miller. Most Americans remember him as the party-switching, twangy-voiced figure who delivered both a nomination speech for Bill Clinton at the Democratic National Convention in 1992 and the ultimate "in your face" nomination speech for George W. Bush at the Republican National Convention in 2004 (and for challenging Chris Matthews to a duel in an interview after the speech).

His critics like to paint Miller as mountaineer with a short fuse and a tendency to blow whichever way the political wind might take him. And to the naïve or most partisan, that would seem the case. But I have dealt with this man at every level—as a Georgia legislator when he was governor, as a foe when I took over the strategy for his opponent in his 1994 re-election campaign, and as a very dear friend from my childhood on.

In 2003 Miller asked me to meet with him in Washington, as a friend, to counsel him on something that he said was very important to him. Once we started talking, it was clear that he had a potential presidential race on his mind. I certainly wasn't an expert on winning Democratic nominations, but I scrambled as fast as I could to put numbers and past history together to figure out how Zell Miller, the conservative Democrat, could win his party's nomination in 2004. That's when he explained that he didn't want the Democratic nomination.

Miller was considering his own third-party run in the 2004 presidential contest. It wasn't out of dislike for George W. Bush; he liked the president immensely. It was instead a result of what he considered a massive drift on the part of the Democratic Party. Miller, who delivered the keynote address at the 1992 Democratic National Convention and who had played a vital role in Bill Clinton's win in that year, felt the national Democratic Party had become far too liberal and out of touch. He resented the gridlock that had taken over the Senate. He disagreed with the rejection of any effort by the Democratic Senate leadership to take more moderate positions on an array of issues. But he has steadfastly refused to change his party affiliation.

Without going into the details of a series of discussions Miller and I had on the subject, it became clear that he was more interested in seeing Congress end its gridlock than in becoming president. Yes, amazingly, the man who just a year later would be delivering another keynote address, this time for the incumbent Republican George W. Bush, could have instead been listed on the ballot in numerous states as his opponent. I believe he thought that a third-party effort might steer conservative Democrats away from the 2004 Democratic nominee, thus both assuring Bush reelection and giving Miller himself a platform to take the national Democrats to the woodshed for a good old-fashioned whupping.

Zell quickly abandoned the idea of running. I was there simply as a friend who happened to be a pollster, knew the GOP landscape, and understood Zell Miller. There was never any doubt in my mind that he would reject consideration of such a move if he thought it would hurt Bush. He abandoned it because of the risks it might pose to the president, but he would have made a very credible and powerful third-party candidate. He would have been a strong candidate not just for his conservative positions, but also for his compassionate zeal over issues that some might have considered liberal, chief among them his desire to bring lasting economic opportunity and quality healthcare and education to the impoverished Black Belt of the South.

To those who lampooned Miller's stern 2004 keynote address to the Republican National Convention, let me give a brief aside. Many considered it a great speech. Others felt it harsh. The political comedians had great fun with it.

But the speech would have shown a softer and wittier Zell Miller had the time allocated for it not been cut at the last minute by those running the convention. He was told to drastically cut the length of his speech, but wasn't given sufficient time to thoughtfully rewrite his remarks. He was forced to deliver his original speech at rapid fire, making funny lines seem harsher and leaving Miller doubting his own effort.

Two days after the speech he called to ask for the "unvarnished truth." "How bad did I hurt the president?" he asked. He had not hurt the president at all, and by the following week he was campaigning in critical swing states. That was on behalf of Bush, not any third-party Zell Miller candidacy.

In 2008 the Republicans had to wonder if one of their own, who had lost faith in the GOP and who did decide to run as a third-party candidate, might have an unusually significant impact on their chances at winning the election.

PART TWO

PARANOID PRECURSORS

★ 11 ★

FROM JFK TO REAGAN:
HOW IT ALL BEGAN

America's true polarization, the idea that one had to be either a Neanderthal stuck in a moral and political time-warp or a flaming liberal, hell-bent on opposing everything from patriotism to Mom's apple pie, started in the 1960s.

For many who were alive at the time of President John Kennedy's assassination, there is continued intrigue over and admiration for the days of Camelot. Baby Boomers, particularly those who grew up in the 1960s, became enamored with the style and grace of the first family. And those who have actually studied JFK's administration in depth understand that, while Kennedy was considered a liberal in areas like the South because of his support for civil rights, he was, in fact, often moderate on many issues.

For example, most people don't realize that JFK was a proponent of tax cuts as a means to stimulate the economy. Those members of Camelot who are still with us would take issue with any attempt to compare Kennedy's rationale for the cut in personal and corporate income tax rates that he advocated in 1963 to that of Ronald Reagan's cuts of the 1980s. Their argument is that Kennedy's proposed cuts were based on the demand-side of the economy versus Reagan's trickle-down approach. There is no better proof than Kennedy's own words, quoted in the *New York Times* in 1962, when he spoke of his proposed tax cut:

"Our true choice is not between tax reduction, on the one hand, and the avoidance of large Federal deficits on the other. It is increasingly clear that, no matter what party is in power, so long as our national security needs keep rising, an economy hampered by restrictive tax rates will never produce enough revenue to balance the budget—just as it will never produce enough jobs or enough profits.

In short, it is a paradoxical truth that tax rates are too high today and tax revenues are too low—and the soundest way to raise revenues in the long run is to cut rates now."

Those who want to fix Kennedy's image to what would today be considered a liberal fail to realize that whether his proposed tax cuts sprung from either the Keynesian (the idea that running a deficit will spur economic growth) or trickle-down schools is of little significance. JFK was a Democrat fighting "restrictive tax rates." That sort of language would hardly sound liberal in 2008. The Kennedys' use of phrases such as "restrictive tax rates" or the word "profits" would likely be removed from any Democratic nominee's speech in 2008, and the "profits" part might not make a Republican candidate's speech, either.

An examination of Kennedy finds him to be an ardent anti-communist with a healthy respect for the military, resulting from his own military service. Kennedy spent much of his thousand days in office in a constant struggle between the two factions of his supporters. In one camp were his powerful allies in Congress who wanted the president to go slow on civil rights, and his top military advisors, who helped get him into hot water with the Bay of Pigs and who pushed for a more hard-line response to Khrushchev during the

Cuban Missile Crisis. In the opposing camp were the more liberal members of his staff, who were obsessed with moving more rapidly to integrate the South, distrusted "big business," and didn't trust the Joint Chiefs of Staff.

But Kennedy was a pragmatist. After the Bay of Pigs fiasco he learned to keep his own counsel in dealing with military confrontations. His decision to attempt to cut tax rates flew directly in the face of some of his more liberal economic advisors. And he paced himself as he moved towards civil rights for African Americans.

By any measure of that era, Kennedy was hardly the flaming liberal that either hardcore segregationists might have accused him of being (segregation being part of the "liberal litmus test" at that time) or which those who carried forth his flame after his death, like his brothers, purported him to have been.

The Kennedy era set the stage for three critical changes in public attitude, which remain in place to this day and which serve as precursors for the 2008 Democratic contest.

First, looks and style matter when it comes to electing our leaders. LBJ was the last president who wasn't, to put it gently, mediagenic. Carter had his white teeth. Reagan had his shock of black hair. Clinton had an obvious way with the ladies. Barrels of ink have been spilled on McCain's square jaw and Obama's athletic build. And while McCain's age and halting motions resulting from the injuries he received in Vietnam might have made a lesser candidate less attractive, his silver hair, stylish wife, and the later emergence of an attractive female running mate would make the overall McCain package equal to the task of Obama, his youthful wife, and his adorable young daughters.

The second and third enduring trends from JFK's era—instantaneous coverage of major news events through television and all the other advancements in communications that followed, and a newfound skepticism on the part of the American people about what they were being told through these new media—both arose out of his controversial assassination.

Survey after survey has shown that Americans continue to view the assassinations of both John Kennedy and Martin Luther King, Jr., among the most significant events of the modern era. The older the respondent is to any poll asking him to name the most important news events of his lifetime, the more likely JFK's assassination is to be either his first or second choice. And among African Americans, King's assassination is obviously a profound and deeply personal event.

Many have noted that broadcast news came of age with its live, continuous coverage of the Kennedy assassination, which included the first live broadcast of a murder, that of Kennedy's accused killer Lee Harvey Oswald, in history.

By the time of King's assassination, JFK's murder had resulted in an ongoing debate among the general public about conspiracy theories.

So what do these two murders have to do with today? They were part of the emergence of full-scale television news and its broadcasting of traumatic events in a ceaseless stream. One might wonder, if the Kennedy assassination had never taken place, how many more years would there have been of simple nightly news broadcasts (still in their infancy) and little live or extended coverage of news events? How many more years would it have taken to reach the concept of 24-hour cable news channels, much less an Internet with uploads of amateur news footage and millions of blogs and websites devoted to the news of the day?

The fear created by such shocking events as the two assassinations and the new ability to cover bad news and to question it instantaneously established the underpinnings of a future "paranoid nation."

★ 12 ★

POPULAR PARANOIAS

In the early part of 2008, the surviving children of Dr. Martin Luther King, Jr. and his deceased wife were embroiled in an intra-family legal squabble about how Dr. King's estate was being handled. This should hardly surprise anyone, given that such tug of war is not uncommon among siblings involved in legacies and estates of value.

After Dr. King's death, his widow, Coretta, and her four children were variously accused of profiting from his death in almost every way imaginable, and seldom were they given sufficient acknowledgment for either the extent of their loss or the mantle of responsibility each of them carried after his death.

The family was maligned, primarily for wanting to be paid for use of Dr. King's speeches and image. Imagine that! They actually believed in free enterprise and the right of inheritance!

In my opinion, the King family—the bearers of the greatest name in African American history, at least until the emergence of Barack Obama—have outshined most other heirs to the rich and famous for commendable behavior, family battles not withstanding.

I should note that not everyone shares my opinion, including the Pulitzer-winning leadership of the editorial board of the King family's hometown *Atlanta Journal-Constitution* newspaper. Given that the paper's editorial board is known to lean in the more liberal and partisan Democratic direction, I found it ironic that the immediate family of Martin Luther King, Jr., often felt greater hostility towards the newspaper's editorial board than did most conservative Republicans. That likely comes as a shock to most in other parts of the nation.

I recall a day in 1994 when Mrs. King, surrounded by her children and supporters, took on her critics at a press conference at the King Center. She called her life's work "a sacred responsibility and legacy borne of tragedy" and denied that anyone in her inner circle was motivated by greed.

"Not even for a moment has personal enrichment been a goal of me or my children," said Mrs. King. "It was not something we wanted, but it is also not something we will turn away from. It seems that the same evil forces that killed Martin Luther King, Jr., are now trying to destroy his family."

The particular controversy at hand was a fight with the National Park Service over management of the MLK National Historic Site, which includes King's birth home and is just up Auburn Avenue from the family-run King Center in Atlanta.

Several years prior to the park controversy, I got to know—and like—the Kings. At the time, they were involved in another dispute, this one involving the possible sale of some of MLK's papers.

I acknowledged that I was in unusual waters when a member of Dr. King's immediate family asked me for advice on the matter. This person did not seek my assistance as an attorney, but only as a friend. I was never asked to keep confidential the beliefs shared with me. But for various reasons, I am now free to share that individual's strong feelings. And I believe that this person's theories about the death of the much-beloved head of his family was undoubtedly shared by many in the immediate family.

It was my impression that many in the family not only believed James Earl Ray innocent of the murder of Martin Luther King, Jr., but they had also lived for years with severe doubt—and even fear—about those they believed to have actually been involved.

These family members suspected several people of being involved with a plot to kill King. Some of King's family also suspected officials at the top of the Federal government. Literally the very top. After all, it's a well-documented fact that the FBI spied on Dr. King and even attempted to coerce him into suicide. That obviously failed, so it stands to reason that some members of the King family might believe that the assassination was Plan B.

And the suspicion, or in some instances, general ill-will for what were considered insincere actions and words at the time of Dr. King's death, did not end with those directly involved in a perceived conspiracy. At least one currently well-known civil rights activist seems, for whatever reason, to have raised family members' eyebrows.

The King family member who confided these frightening theories is incapable of stepping forward to admit any of these personal beliefs publically. Since my discussions both Mrs. King and her daughter Yolanda have passed away. And it is likely that no member of the family will ever name the names that I heard in conjunction with at least one other prominent past leader as I listened to the phenomenal and detailed version of the plot to kill Dr. King that was told to my colleague and me over a period of several months.

Regardless of how they are sometimes characterized in the press, members of the King family are most assuredly not crazy. And the family knows that mainstream America would receive news of a conspiracy theory from the King family to be evidence that they'd gone over the edge. But such thoughts serve as a reminder that concern, fear, or paranoia, whether based on fact or conjecture, know no political, philosophical, or racial boundaries. And I must say I believed their story and do to this day.

My acquaintance with the family made me realize two important things: that not everyone who believes in a conspiracy theory is an obsessed wing nut and that, just as importantly, at least some major events which take place in America—such as those in the turbulent 1960s—could actually theoretically be the result of a multitude of complex interests and sophisticated entities and individuals. Whether they act in concert or out of coincidence is the matter debated every time that unexpectedly bad things happen to prominent Americans or to America itself.

The assassinations of Kennedy and King helped establish a sort of conspiracy mindset that later morphed into a general skepticism and jaded perspective, which now permeates almost every aspect of life in America.

While a Department of Justice Report in 2000 was issued to debunk "recent allegations regarding the assassination of Dr. Martin Luther King," the last and only official inquiry into both the murders of Kennedy and King was conducted in 1978 by a special select Committee of the U.S. House, which determined that, in both cases, the victims were killed most likely as the result of conspiracies involving more than one individual.

Does that necessarily mean a conspiracy existed in both cases? Absolutely not.

Since the 1970s, science has advanced, and many respected journalists and scholars have provided, strong arguments against either murder having been the result of anything more than the actions of mentally disturbed lone gunmen. The truth is, there are no definitive answers. But when there are no answers, strange coincidences and questionable motives can lead to justifiably strong conjecture.

From alleged electronic ballot machines being rigged to a Michael Moore concept of 9/11, America has been led down a path of paranoia. In the instance of Dr. King, paranoia was born from the blood he shed, the devastated family he left behind, and an emerging African American community in America that, in 1968, felt something just didn't add up.

It's not hard to comprehend a prominent African American family having doubts over the murder of their father, who was, in the last few years of his life, considered by his own government as a threat and, perhaps, revolutionary. But some people—many more than you'd probably guess—actually believe that a secret society of elite powerbrokers plan and control each and every aspect of our lives and have, in fact, done so throughout history. This rather substantial sub-culture, composed of everything from left-wing fringe elements to ultraconservatives, believe "the government" is controlled by a small, elite group that manages and manipulates the public's knowledge of various issues.

Talk to the conspiracy theorists awhile, and you'll hear a lot of things. Unbelievable things.

They'll tell you, with absolutely straight faces, that these unseen Svengalis—Dick Cheney supposedly is one of the few whose role is publicly known—taunt us by leaving clues of their existence in plain sight. These seeming paranoids see evidence in everything from the eye and pyramid on the one-dollar bill to the acronym for the North Atlantic Treaty Organization—NATO—which can be rearranged to spell Aton, the sun god in Egyptian mythology. In the world of the conspiracy theorist, that has meaning.

Although such things must take up an awful amount of their time, the elite also find time to make lots of money, ensure that the world is perpetually at war, and keep a tight lid on such "facts" as the so-called Roswell crash of an alleged alien spaceship.

It is a reality that certain facts, such as the coincidence of the Bush family being a part of the Carlisle Group, a New York investment group whose members include the Bin Laden family, add up in the heads of some and fuel a rather potent world of conspiracy subgroups.

Ignore them if you want, but they are there, and not all of them look like crazies. Trust me, you know some of them even though you don't know you know them: a neighbor mowing his lawn with a frown on his face because he just noticed a jet overhead and believes the contrail behind it is a chemical being released by the government to control the masses; the security guard at your bank, who, if you engage him in conversation, will tell you with certainty that plans for a single-world economy are already underway and will erase the borders between the United States, Canada, and Mexico; the history teacher at your kid's high school who is convinced the government plans to put computerized tracking chips in the head of every American, and that the chips have not only been developed, but are already being manufactured, probably by Halliburton.

Start talking to people you come in contact with every day, and you'll find out I'm right.

Oh, yeah. And do a few Google searches while you're at it. You can start by typing in "Truth Movement."

This is hardly the only group of conspiracy theorists out there—they're actually called CTs, by the way—but they are one of the largest, and one to which an enormous number of Americans subscribe, in whole or in part.

"The 9/11 Truth Movement is the name adopted by organizations and individuals that question the mainstream account of the September 11, 2001, attacks against the United States," according to a Wikipedia entry. "Movement members communicate primarily through the Internet and regularly convene for local meetings, national and international conferences, and public demonstrations."

It's appropriate to continue to quote the definition of the Truth Movement from this Wiki site, the collaborative Web format tailor-made for the paranoid: "Frequently expressed propositions among movement supporters are that the mainstream account of the events of 9/11 is false and that the perceived anomalies in the official account can better be explained by the theory that a 'rogue network,' including individuals in the U.S. government, planned, carried out, and covered up the attack or deliberately allowed the attacks to take place."

Interesting, if nothing else.

These concerned citizens spend an inordinate amount of time connecting the dots—all the dots, some real and some imagined. Most of them believe the Masons are involved, of course, but they don't stop there. They can take any world event in the twenty-first century, say, the Federal Emergency Management Agency's poor response to Hurricane Katrina, and rationalize some connection to the Illuminati and the Knights Templar.

Oh, and a great many of them are also convinced that the world will come to an end in the year 2012. We can blame that on the ancient Mayans. They organized a calendar which had several cycles, the last of which will end in December of 2012.

"There are dozens of theories about how this might happen," notes an entry in the website howstuffworks.com. "Some claim that 2012 is when the Earth will experience a polar shift. Others say that after 2012, the Earth will experience a period of terrible destruction followed by a new age of peace and enlightenment. A few claim that in 2012, a secret government will accomplish its goal of total world domination. What will actually happen? Check back with us on Jan. 1, 2013."

There have always been people who believed that the end of the world is coming. And, so far, they've always been wrong. What's changed is that, in the twenty–first century, these very paranoid individuals are no longer isolated. They don't have to lecture from soap boxes or publish their beliefs on handbills. Now, they have the Internet. They all have their own blogs and websites, and they correspond with one another. And, as they swap new conspiracy theories, their paranoia builds and builds.

But something else happens, too.

The fact that other people are saying the same things, often on well-designed websites, in professional looking "documentaries," and occasionally in legitimate lecture forums, convinces them that they are correct.

Although these may well be people who need to be on significant medication, it would be folly to pretend they don't exist. Why? Because there are more of them than you can possibly imagine.

The so-called legitimate media has barely noticed their existence, let alone reported on it, but the citizens of this Paranoid Nation are an emerging power. The concept that someone, somewhere is up to something had become a near mantra by the time our nation entered the twenty-first century. And when more concrete and serious issues are to be considered, the subgroup of those who believe that there are powerful forces impacting their lives grows and begins to include the nation's best-known leaders and celebrities.

Hillary Clinton felt a "vast, right-wing conspiracy" was out to bring down her husband's presidency. Michael Moore won an Academy Award through the clever juxtaposition of file film footage, suggesting conspiratorial actions by the Bush administration surrounding 9/11 and the war in Iraq. And before that there was a famous "Florida recount" in 2000. And, on the other side of the political spectrum, more than one bestseller, such as Bernard Goldberg's book about the media, *Bias: A CBS Insider Exposes How the Media Distort the News*, has outlined liberal conspiracies in the media. Troubled leaders in the Republican Party—and, unfortunately, there have been more than a few—cried that they were victims of, well, a vast left-wing conspiracy. Even Republican members of Congress are suspect of the Bush administration's modus operandi when it comes to implementing the war in Iraq and in dealing straight with them on an endless number of issues where transparency has been replaced by a shroud of secrecy. Even in the midst of the last days of the 2008 election, Bob Woodward was detailing his story of how President Bush, facing the 2006 midterm elections, told the American people that the nation was winning the war in Iraq even as he received private briefings that the war, at that point, was being lost. Conspiracy or expediency?

What did fringe conspiracy theories, combined with more legitimate concerns or assertions from prominent families, political leaders, and journalists, have to do with the 2008 race for the White House? More than most would admit.

The 2008 race had two clouds hanging over it from the beginning. One was a low-boiling fear of another attack on the order of 9/11, or at the very least, a belief that Republicans would use terror as a means of scaring voters into their camp in the late days of the campaign. The other was a concern for the personal safety of one of the candidates, Barack Obama. Both fears, following the CTs' view, were created by those unseen elites: small groups of people who wanted to influence the election or, as is more generally believed, outside forces with a desire to assert their influence and power through terror during this most significant of campaigns.

When McCain adviser Charlie Black, a longtime GOP operative, speculated that an act of terrorism during the campaign season would be, from a strategic standpoint, a boost for the Republican nominee, the blogosphere was alive with accusations of planned attacks and fear-mongering on the part of Republicans. It was hard to decide if the greater degree of paranoia was among Republicans who feared such an event or those who believed that Fahrenheit 911 would repeat itself.

In September of 2008, during an on-air commentary, controversial cable news personality Keith Olbermann accused the campaign of John McCain of pandering to the "paranoia" over the 2001 terrorist attacks. The term "paranoia" was alive and well to the very end of the 2008 race.

The first major African American candidate for president was most active in the black community, where, from preachers to activists to average citizens, the worry for his safety was perceived as very real. But why? Perhaps understanding the real beliefs of some of the icons of the Civil Rights Movement helps explain the paranoia that clouded the campaign. Perhaps the memories of John F. Kennedy and Martin Luther King, Jr., lingered in their minds.

Add to that Robert Kennedy, who was viewed as the member of his family most sympathetic towards the Civil Rights Movement. Late in the 2008 season, in explaining why she was continuing her primary fight long after it seemed plausible that she could win the nomination, Hillary Clinton mentioned the fact that the fight for the Democratic nomination in 1968 had stretched right down to the last contests partly because of the assassination of Bobby Kennedy earlier in the campaign season.

Her remarks caused an uproar. Clinton quickly declared that she in no way intended to insinuate that harm could come to Obama. But from a strategic standpoint, that seemed like the opposite of her intended message. The comment prompted a slew of articles expressing security fears for the man who seems, according to Robert Kennedy's widow Ethel, so much like her late husband.

In the end, the "calamity" feared by Democrats in the form of terrorism would instead be economic and would hurt the Republicans. Barack Obama would remain safe throughout the campaign, although he would be increasingly compared to JFK and RFK.

But, another political figure mirrored Obama more closely. His experience had been mostly in state government, he too had written a book prior to launching his candidacy, he was an outsider, and, like Barack Obama, he was viewed as the least viable in the field when he sought the presidency. That political figure was Jimmy Carter.

★ 13 ★

DON'T LOOK HIM IN THE EYES:
THE STRANGE TALE OF
JIMMY CARTER

By the time the 2008 election reached maturation, the comparisons of Barack Obama to various leaders such as JFK or Robert Kennedy began to include comparisons to another underdog presidential candidate. He was a candidate who rose seemingly from nowhere to captivate the American public with the uniqueness of his background (Southern) and his youthful charisma. His name was Jimmy Carter.

In its September 1, 2008, edition *Newsweek* profiled Barack Obama in a piece entitled, "A Liberal's Lament." The article declared the obvious when it said that, "Obama resembles Jimmy Carter more than he does any other Democratic president in living memory."

Here's a true confession. Although my admiration for Ronald Reagan is immense, and I earned the right to have it by truly being there during the Reagan Revolution, the first vote I ever cast for president was for Jimmy Carter in 1980. Although I was working for Republican senatorial candidate Mack Mattingly and U.S. Representative Newt Gingrich and believed that the GOP offered a fresh approach, and I had become enthralled with Reagan, I could not bring myself to vote against a president, a real live president who I had actually observed, listened to, and had been around as a young boy. I doubted I would ever be around another in my lifetime, and at age twenty, my longstanding Georgia roots overrode my newfound Republican devotion.

There's a real lesson here. As the 2008 campaign advanced and issues of gender or race arose, I constantly heard critics say "that person is voting for him only because he is black" or "she's supporting her because she's a woman." Well duh? It's hard for people who feel a special bond—be it gender, race, or region-based—to turn on that special connection.

In his 1979 *Who is Running America?: The Carter Years*, political science professor Thomas Dye asserts that Jimmy Carter was recruited and sponsored to run for president by those close to David Rockefeller and the leadership elite in America. Carter might have been the Democratic elite's chosen candidate, but he was an outsider coming into a town that truly hates outsiders. And he was entering a city—and a nation—in retreat.

Many of my Republican friends with whom I shared the years of Reagan, Bush, and Gingrich didn't realize that much of the economic disaster with which Carter had to contend upon taking office was the remnant of desperate efforts by Nixon and Ford to heal an economy crippled by the costs of the Vietnam War and Lyndon Johnson's entitlement programs. Let's be fair, who would the conservative of 2008 consider more "conservative": Nixon, who actually imposed wage and price controls, created the EPA and OSHA (despised by many conservatives), and first implemented affirmative action set-asides? Or was it Carter, who deregulated the entire airline industry?

And by the way, much of that cool automated weaponry that introduced "surgical strike" into the popular lexicon, also used by Bush 41 in the original Gulf War, can be credited to Carter. Although it's true that Carter allowed our conventional weapons to dwindle and turn rusty, the former Navy man insisted on the use of defense research and development of technologies that reduced risk to humans. Airborne drones and the like were not the result of the influence of Star Wars. They were the result of Jimmy Carter's engineering background.

The ultimate causes of the Iranian hostage crisis, the issue that drove him out of office, could hardly be blamed on Carter: the fall of Mohammed Reza Shah Pahlavi in the Iranian Revolution of 1979, which led to the rise of the Ayatollah Khomeini and the overrun of the U.S. embassy in Tehran. Carter was as adamant a supporter of the Shah as his GOP predecessors had been. Both Democrats and Republicans knew that the Shah was a cruel despot, but at least he was a pro-American despot. And if anyone doubts the seriousness of Carter's efforts to end the hostage standoff, I refer them to one of the best modern political diaries written, that of former Carter Chief of Staff, the late Hamilton Jordan, entitled, *Crisis.*

Jordan engaged in a daring effort of negotiations that included a need for him to wear an elaborate disguise while meeting with dangerous go-betweens in attempting to negotiate the freedom of the hostages. In fact, Carter and his team had basically negotiated the terms of a release of the hostages, but their captors chose to hold them prisoner until just moments after Ronald Reagan was sworn into office. It was the captors' final poke at a demoralized Carter administration as it exited Washington.

Most conservatives, and even a healthy percentage of moderates view Carter's presidency as an utter and complete failure, and they mock his sometimes over-the-top and increasingly liberal post-presidency. But they should be mindful that Generations X and Y are too young to remember the double-digit inflation of his presidency or the abortive effort to send a military strike force to rescue the Iranian hostages. They know nothing of the ridicule that was hurled towards his seemingly countrified and somewhat eccentric family, mostly by a media that loved abusing Carter's southern heritage.

And most young Americans don't recall the Carter energy crisis, his often lampooned "cardigan sweater speech," his description of America as being in a "malaise," or his self-admitted underestimation of the Soviets before they invaded Afghanistan.

Nor will most older Americans want to recall that Jimmy Carter was pushing for alternative energy sources thirty years before surveys would show that a majority of Americans want a comprehensive energy plan designed to include advanced technological versions of the very alternatives Carter advocated.

The difference in opinions over Carter as president are a simple matter of young versus old. For older Americans Jimmy Carter was, as some had observed, like an order of sweet and sour pork. You liked half of the taste and didn't like the other. But you knew darn well you didn't want to risk eating it after it had been out too long.

The contemporary acts of former president Carter (a.k.a. Saint Jimmy) are so emblazoned in the minds of younger voters, among those under the age of forty who our polling firm surveyed, Carter jumps from being among the least admired presidents in modern history to one of the most admired former presidents.

Once again my Gump side gave me a glimpse at Carter before, during, and after his presidency. As an English lesson, our fourth-grade class was required to write a "business letter." At the time, Georgia's infamous segregationist governor, Lester Maddox, was in the hospital for treatment of one of his many maladies. I didn't know Maddox, of course, and my parents had actually supported his GOP opponent. But he was governor, and I was attracted to politics, so my carefully written little letter went off, presumably to the pro forma stack of correspondence that all elected officials receive.

Several weeks later, as we sat at our family dinner table, the phone rang. My father answered, and I could tell by his hesitance that he was confused about the call. "May I ask who is calling?" I heard him say.

Then he turned to me, obviously having recognized the unmistakable rasp, and said, "Matt, Lester Maddox is on the phone for you."

Maddox, was known for reaching out to people—and, yes, sometimes with an axe handle. Fortunately he never actually hit anyone. I don't think it was in him to physically harm anyone. Somehow he was moved to respond to my letter, not with just a pro forma letter of his own, but with a phone call.

Even though I'm a guy who in later years was a contributor to the Georgia Black Legislative Caucus; who worked with families of civil rights leaders; and who occupied an office next to former Atlanta Mayor and Ambassador Andrew Young, it's no surprise that, at a young age Maddox's stance on race flew over my head.

Sadly, I later knew Maddox well enough to know what many African American leaders who served with him knew, too: that he got along better with most blacks than with most whites. Why? Because Maddox had grown up desperately poor and identified with those who were underprivileged. In his later years, I tried to reach out and explain Maddox's true philosophy in an interview I had with him for my column a year or so before his death.

In the interview, Maddox said he was sorry if any of his actions in the 1960s hurt anyone's feelings—including African Americans. But after the column was published (and he caught hell from some of his old-time friends), he recanted his statement and became temporarily upset with me. His family knew his heart and told me they had appreciated me capturing their dad's true spirit— which was much kinder than the way he was portrayed in the media. I wish he had stuck to the words that came from his heart that day of the interview. I wish he, like his contemporary George Wallace, had apologized—not for believing in states' rights—but for hurting people, mainly African Americans, with some of his words and actions during the turbulent years of the 1960s.

When I was a child Maddox took a true liking to me, and I became a sort of young permanent fixture, first in his governor's office, where I was made an honorary lieutenant colonel of his staff, and later as his "permanent page" as he served as lieutenant governor presiding over Georgia's Senate. Maddox's staff allowed me the run of his office suites. And that brings me to Jimmy Carter.

In January 1971 Jimmy Carter, a fresh-faced and progressive state senator from Plains, was sworn in as Maddox's successor. Governor Maddox had invited me to be with his family as they greeted the Carters. I was, of course, just another kid—there was a handshake, maybe a photo, now lost. We proceeded out to the balcony of Georgia's ornate capitol building where I sat with the Maddox group as the two were sworn in. Maddox, term-limited to one four-year stint, ran for lieutenant governor and won easily.

But a funny thing happened, which allowed me to have a continual inside view of Carter, who I otherwise did not know. In Georgia in those days, key support staffers, such as those who manned the desk in the anteroom outside the governor's office, never really changed jobs. To my wonderment, all of my old pals who had treated this young kid with such kindness were all still there in the Carter administration. So, being the precocious child I was, I continued my routine of hanging out right outside the governor's personal office whenever I could leave school early or in the summers.

Let it be clear that Carter likely had no use for a kid just sitting around his office. I'm sure he never even knew my name. But I watched him carefully. The first thing I noticed was obvious—he was far more serious and to the point than the flamboyant Maddox, who had been known to ride his bicycle backwards on the grounds of the Governor's Mansion. The door to Carter's office was usually closed and there was neither the chaos nor the throngs of people who had surrounded Maddox.

Even as an eleven-year-old, I could see that Carter was charismatic and quick to smile with the public, but could be icily cold and tough when surrounded by his closest associates. I wouldn't want this assessment to disappoint fans of Carter. Make no mistake that no one ever reaches the top in the world of politics without a degree of toughness and self-confidence bordering on egotism. Even Carter would likely admit that.

One book on the Carter presidency suggested that he always insisted that no one working in the White House—the executive mansion staff and the like—was to make eye contact with the First Family. My friends, who basically ran the place, say that was an out-and-out lie. But everyone who really knew Carter could tell you that he could run hot and cold. And when he went cold, you knew it.

I remember the first time it struck me that Carter had higher ambitions. It was towards the end of his four-year run as governor. The General Assembly of the Organization of American States came to Atlanta to meet in 1974. It was the first time the General Assembly had met outside a national capital, and it was a big deal. I was there when his staff cleared Carter's few personal items from his official office, because he had offered it for use by Secretary of State Henry Kissinger. After the meetings I heard several staffers talking about how impressed Kissinger had been with Carter. Clearly something was up. But I was too young and out of the loop to realize just how big "up" was.

It was really later in my years dealing with D.C. politics and as an attorney that some of my estimations about Carter were confirmed. One of his most senior White House aides told me of a time when he and President Carter were discussing some matter over which the aide felt quite passionate. "Mr. President, I strongly urge you to do this," he said. He told me that Carter looked up at him and said, "You never 'strongly urge' the president of the United States to do anything."

And Carter could send a message. After he left office, Carter wanted a road built to his new presidential library in Atlanta, but the original path would cut through a key neighborhood in the electoral district of a state senator with whom Carter was very close. This prominent individual was known for having tromped through the snow in New Hampshire campaigning for the then-Democratic underdog in 1976. But because of the adamant opposition of the senator's constituents to the road that would slice through their neighborhood, he had been forced to oppose it.

Carter had a long memory. Years later, that same senator took his young boy to a Christmas gathering at the Carter Center. A line of people formed, hoping to have their photographs taken with the former president. After waiting for some time, the senator and his child made their way to the front of the line. There were still many people behind them waiting. President and Mrs. Carter abruptly stood up and left.

Because of my past years as an active Republican, I have an unusual view of both those who see Carter as a failed president (for my money, others certainly more readily qualify for the prize of worst president in modern times) and those who revere his post-presidential accomplishments.

Having known so many of his top associates, it was always my feeling that Carter was a man lured into the presidency by the nation's political and business establishment, only to be abandoned by the same people. Why? Some familiar with those times say that it was so very clear after Gerald Ford's pardon of Nixon that the Watergate hangover could make Ford's reelection problematic. The so-called "Elite" could not risk the rise of a Democrat with whom they had no connection or ability to guide. Hedging their bets with Carter, who would definitely need their assistance if elected, seemed a smart move.

The treatment of Carter's family and administration, particularly the group the press termed the "Georgia Mafia," was not only condescending but bordered on the absurd. With then-Speaker of the House Tip O'Neill nipping at him and Sen. Ted Kennedy planning to challenge his incumbency in 1980, Carter was never, in my judgment, given the opportunity to find his bearings in the Oval Office.

I once gave my assessment of the Carter administration's relationship with the Washington Establishment that so completely rejected his outsider administration to a longtime associate of President Carter. The Carter intimate said, "Yes, you're right, but we could have reached out to them more. We just didn't understand until it was too late."

Has Carter become too liberal in his golden years? Probably so. Has he shot his mouth off in recent years to grab headlines? Arguably. But no one can deny that Carter has likely been the most productive and active former president in American history. And that is how an increasing number of Americans will remember him.

All this, too, is a precursor to 2008. In so many ways Barack Obama seemed like a fresh-faced Jimmy Carter addressing the unspoken or politely posited question looming over the campaign. In 1976 it was, "Will America elect a southerner to the White House?" In 2008 it was, "Will America elect a black man to the White House?" Obama, much like Carter, seemed imbued with charisma and the promise of a change.

Few realize that the man who would bring the greatest change to American politics since Franklin Roosevelt almost didn't win his battle to become the fortieth president of the United States. Carter pollster Pat Caddell showed the race still tight in many critical states going into the last week of the election. There was rampant speculation in the media that a deal to free the Iranian hostages was imminent. Had the deal been struck, there was significant polling to suggest that Carter might have defeated Ronald Reagan. But it was not to be. And even Republicans, many of whom were weary of their nominee, had no idea what was to come.

★ 14 ★

THE HERO THEY NEVER WANTED:
RONALD REAGAN AND THE
TRUE CONSERVATIVES

In the late 1970s and into 1980, Republicans could sense that Jimmy Carter's executive stumblings or misfortunes might have opened the door to the Republicans, even so close on the heels of Nixon's alleged crimes and Gerald Ford's pardon of them.

It seems incredible now, but in 1980, it was hard to find anyone in the Republican establishment who wanted Ronald Reagan to be their party's nominee for president. Nine out of ten Republican "Establishment" activists who were around in those days would be bold-faced liars if they said otherwise. Does that surprise you? Well certainly, because Reagan's success as president was so overwhelming that no one wants to admit the real story of 1980. But there are some of us who will eagerly tell it.

Approaching the election of 1980, the Republican establishment was split between two very different men, both of whom had something big in common: Texas.

The faction known as the Rockefeller Republicans, the moderates who were more interested in power than in ideology, were backing George H. W. Bush, a former Texas Congressman who had served as ambassador to the United Nations, Chairman of the Republican National Committee, Director of the Central

Intelligence Agency, and head of the Council on Foreign Relations. There wasn't much doubt that the Ford/Kissinger side of the GOP upper leadership felt comfortable with Bush, especially his presumed ability to beef up America's military and repair foreign affairs after Carter's mistakes.

Moreover, the Democrats had allowed Idaho Senator Frank Church to open up to the public a full investigation of the secret world of intelligence. (Church had fought against Carter for the 1976 Democratic nomination.) The Church Committee's actions led to constraints on the way the CIA is run. Consequently, Republican kingpins felt it necessary to get "The Company" back in order. Bush's experience as chief of the CIA in 1976 and 1977 made him doubly desirable for this reason.

But there was another establishment candidate, one who the media thought to be an outsider with only one discernable political skill—the ability to raise money. His name was John Connally. The former governor of Texas still retained national name recognition as the conservative Democrat (later Republican) who was riding in John Kennedy's presidential limousine on that fateful Dallas day in November 1963.

Why Connally as a candidate? Well, some of it goes back to, of all people, Richard Nixon. By 1980 Nixon had begun to emerge from his self-imposed internal exile and was a quiet but constant entertainer of powerful political dinner guests. While I'm sure Nixon has written twenty different versions of who he wanted as the party's nominee in 1980, the fact is that he was instrumental in convincing key supporters, particularly in the South, where he remained popular in the party, that only Connally was electable. And it worked. Some of the biggest donors to the GOP filled "Big John's" coffers.

What is today a dirty little secret is that back in 1980 one could support Bush, Connally, or even the new senate superstar, Senate Minority Leader Howard Baker of Tennesessee, who had risen to national prominence during the televised Watergate hearings. But if one wanted to be with the "in" Republicans, the "cool group," one didn't dare give any credence to the name Reagan.

Much of this attitude towards Reagan was a result of his having dared to challenge the incumbent Republican President Gerald Ford, a darling of the GOP's so-called "Rockefeller wing," in 1976 (this despite Nelson Rockefeller having been basically dumped from the ticket in 1980). But some of this attitude was a result of the fact that most of these longtime Republican stalwarts really didn't buy into the Reagan philosophy. After all, it was George H. W. Bush who called Reagan's supply-side approach to tax cutting "voodoo economics." And in muted conversations, there were fears that the cowboy Reagan might have an itchy trigger finger when it came to dealing with the nation's biggest international foes, particularly the powerful Soviet Union.

That just goes to show how far off the mark so-called political insiders can be! The earliest contest in 1980 gave Bush supporters a strong belief that their man could win it all. But the turning point for Reagan came at a debate in Nashua, New Hampshire, when it seemed that all of his opponents were ganging up on him in a concerted Old Line GOP effort to nominate "Anyone but Ronnie." The moderator of the *Nashua Telegraph*-sponsored debate ordered Reagan's microphone turned off because he was "out of order" based on the rules the candidates had agreed to. A red-faced Reagan shouted, in a paraphrase of a line from the Frank Capra film *State of the Union*, "I am paying for this microphone, Mr. Green!" Regardless of the candidate's small gaffe (the editor's name was, in fact, Jon Breen), the crowd went wild. Instantly one sensed that the age-old concept that the GOP always nominated, if not the "chosen" establishment candidate, one who could easily be controlled, was dead. The man who'd fired the fatal shot was Ronald Reagan.

Not that the Old Line group, still pinning their hopes on George H. W. Bush, planned to go away quietly. Understand that some of what I'm about to write has been handed down over the years by various names you would immediately recognize (although not Newt Gingrich), and, as is often the case, the full behind-the-scenes story can't be proved. Moreover, none of Reagan's supporters would ever admit to it. But trust me, it happened.

The 1980 Republican National Convention was held in Detroit, in the home state of then-Reagan nemesis President Gerald Ford. Make no mistake, Ford was still sore at Reagan for having challenged him in 1976 for the GOP presidential nomination.

The Bush Old Liners wanted to keep from being shut out of what looked like at least a possible Reagan presidency. Unlike on the Democratic side, the Republican vice presidency has often been used as a means of keeping the Old Guard in the center of things. Those who really know the GOP know to steer clear of that trap, hence Nixon's out-of-the-blue choice of the harmless Spiro Agnew for vice president in 1968. But with the political guns being pointed to his head, Nixon named the consummate insider, Ford, as his "chosen" replacement after Agnew resigned early into Nixon's second term.

This trend continued with Ford rewarding the party's ultimate Old Liner and oft-considered "insider" alternative to Nixon, Nelson Rockefeller, with the vice presidency in 1974. The Old Liners' unspoken rule was "if we can't control the presidency outright, we can at least own an interest in the presidency."

Shortly before the 1980 convention, Ronald Reagan was looking at a host of names for his running mate when the name of Gerald Ford suddenly popped up. It was basically unheard of—a former president running to be vice president. As the concept began to leak to the press at the Detroit convention, Reagan swiftly learned through back channels the heavy price he would have to pay for his dream ticket. Ford wanted basic control of foreign policy with Henry Kissinger back in his old day job as secretary of state, and strong monetary control with Ford's friend and trusted advisor Alan

Greenspan as head of the Department of the Treasury. I had to chuckle when I saw pictures of Kissinger holding court at the 2008 Republican Convention in St. Paul. While Kissinger would have people believe he has little interest in or knowledge of party politics, he could, in years past, be found casually observing the goings on at the GOP National Conventions, as he did when we entertained him in Gingrich's suite in 1996 where Newt was the presiding officer of the convention.

Reagan allowed formal negotiations between Ford's people and his own to continue at the convention but was stunned when he heard Gerald Ford in a live interview with television legend Walter Cronkite. Ford implied that he was amenable to an agreement that basically amounted to a co-presidency, to use the term seized upon by commentators to describe the potential ticket.

Enter Richard V. Allen, the man who would later become Reagan's first National Security Director. Allen is a controversial figure in that he not only detailed the Reagan-Ford potential deal in writing years later, but also because he was the source of a rather unflattering version of former Secretary of State Al Haig's performance the day Ronald Reagan was shot in 1981.

While Allen was certainly loyal to Reagan, having served as his foreign policy advisor for years prior to the 1980 campaign, he nevertheless had strong ties back to the Nixon White House and plenty of members of the inner circle who ranked above him in those earlier days. In other words, he was the perfect potential conduit to introduce Bush as a last-minute alternative to Ford as vice president.

By his own admission, Allen did just that on the night that the frenzy over naming Ford the VP nominee swept through Cobo Arena in Detroit. But is there more to Allen's story? Many GOP old-timers believe that floating Ford as vice president was a ruse. Basically, it was a squeeze play which forced Reagan to seek someone from the Establishment wing of the party, and on darn short notice. By 11:00 PM on the night of the Cronkite-Ford interview, the convention hall was almost out of control with excitement in anticipation of a joint Reagan-Ford appearance. Reagan knew he had to pull the trigger and stop the deal. He asked Bush to be his vice president.

It was no secret that Reagan wasn't wild about Bush. And it's doubtful whether Bush's name would have come up so swiftly in the absence of Allen's presence with Reagan throughout the entire night's ordeal. To be fair, there are highly credible Reagan intimates, such as former Attorney General Ed Meese, who to this day dispute the Allen version of what happened that night at the convention. But regardless of whose story is the complete truth, the rushed timing indicated how important keeping a lid on the various powers within the Republican party was to all involved. The event would foreshadow similar concerns over the 2008 vice presidential selection.

And what did the inner circle lose by not having Ford on the ticket? In the short term, a few key cabinet posts. But in the long run, nothing. The likely reality is that Gerald Ford had no interest in being vice president. And in short order, Bush's close friend Senator James Baker would move in to control not only foreign policy, but much of the Reagan White House.

It's ironic that Reagan's two genuine qualifications to naming Bush to his ticket that night were, first, that he embrace the GOP platform, which was "pro-life." This was an issue that the moderate Bush had danced around for years. And Reagan also insisted that Bush accept the so called trickle-down economic philosophy of using tax cuts to stimulate the economy.

Gossip maven Kitty Kelley is not always viewed as the best of sources, but I find her description of Nancy Reagan on that pivotal evening the best at capturing the mood of the Reagans toward the Bushes. The author contends that, as Ronald Reagan addressed the Republican Convention and announced his decision to name Bush as his running mate, Nancy Reagan nearly fell apart. "She looked vulnerable . . . unable to hold back her tears," Kelley wrote. "She hated the idea of George Bush on the ticket."

The next day, when the Bushes met with the Reagans in the Reagans' suite at the convention, Barbara Bush, according to Kelley, disarmed Ronald Reagan by embracing him and saying, "We are going to work our tails off for you."

But Kelley goes on to report, "Mrs. Bush would have a more difficult time charming the candidate's wife, for Nancy Reagan was not so easily beguiled as her husband and already disliked the silver-haired aristocrat who was so sure of her place in the world."

Throughout their eight years in the White House, Nancy Reagan would come to embrace many a top adviser brought to the Reagan Administration through association with George Bush. But, symbolic of a large portion of those Republicans who always feel like outsiders around the Northeastern elite wing of the GOP, she refused to embrace George Bush.

Mrs. Reagan—whose reported nickname for Bush was "Whiney"—made it clear that she felt the vice president was never fully on board with Reagan's political philosophy and that he failed to assist her and others in the administration in removing Chief of Staff Donald Regan once he went out of control.

It's telling that Nancy Reagan barely campaigned for George Bush. And when Bush won election in 1988 without her help, Mrs. Reagan left the White House reportedly unhappy. This smart woman was well aware that the party had been taken back by the very establishment which had attempted to lock her husband out for many years.

Mrs. Reagan's well-known desire to protect her husband was never clearer than during a speech he gave to a large Republican gathering more than a year after he left office. A small group of his supporters gathered in a holding room before escorting the president to the dining room where he was to give his speech. In the elevator he looked every bit as strong and imposing as he ever had. He had not lost the charisma, the aura that one felt in his presence.

Holding an advance copy of his speech in my hand, I then went to my table in the dining room to sit with my wife.

The GOP's greatest hero was doing what he did best: giving a fantastic speech to over a thousand seated guests. Then it happened. He decided to veer off his teleprompter. It started with a joke. The blood drained from Mrs. Reagan's face. President Reagan got through the set-up and then, after a pause, simply said, "You know, I've forgotten how this ends." He struggled for the punch line, but it never came.

Things went downhill. At one point, still rambling away from his written remarks, Reagan went so far as to say something like "when Al Smith was president." For those who don't recall their history classes, Al Smith was the 1928 Democratic candidate for president, but he got trounced by Republican Herbert Hoover.

Overall, the event ended well. But we never saw Ronald Reagan in person again. Just a few years later he released a statement acknowledging that he was a victim of Alzheimer's.

When it's all said and done, the benchmark for the Republicans will always be Ronald Reagan. He is to modern-day Republicans what Roosevelt and Kennedy (and, to some, Clinton) are to Democrats. But most GOP big shots of the late 1970s and even the early 1980s would be lying if they claimed either that Reagan was their candidate in the 1980 primary, or that they could easily have imagined that years later, when planes landed at D.C.'s national airport, the flight attendants would be welcoming passengers to the Ronald Reagan National Airport.

★ 15 ★

"DELAYING" A CAREER:
HOW A HAMMER CLEARED THE WAY
FOR GEORGE W. BUSH

One might wonder why untold tales of George H. W. Bush's reelection effort, the rise and fall of Newt Gingrich as speaker of the House, and the pathway opened for George W. Bush to win the GOP nomination in 2000 would be critical to understanding the mysteries of the 2008 presidential contest. In fact, the stories are essential, not only in seeing the patterns that repeat themselves over and over, but in determining the players on the political stage who would reassert themselves in 2008.

Consider the article written by John Feehery, who worked with the House Republican leadership from 1989 until 2005, which appeared in the online edition of Politico the weekend after Congress passed what would become known as "the Wall Street-to-Main Street" bailout in the last few weeks of the 2008 election.

Feehery notes, "I have been to this rodeo before. House Republicans are in full revolt. A prominent leader condemns harshly a plan put forward by the president. Dire consequences are promised if action is not taken. Wall Street brokers warn about the market implications. Other Republicans cry treachery and warn about the march to socialism. Is it 2008 or 1990? To me, this is déjà vu all over again."

Feehery goes on to describe the 1990 battle between Newt Gingrich and George H. W. Bush over Bush's decision to back a move by Democratic Congressional members to raise taxes as the nation's recession continued to deepen. The history of those events is critical in understanding both the irony and implications of the events that were to unfold some eighteen years later.

President George Bush (we all added the H. W. later, after George W. was elected) seems to be about as nice a guy as you would ever want to meet. Sure, he has a patrician background and feels most comfortable with those with whom he's familiar, those who his son perhaps only half-jokingly referred to at a 2000 New York City fundraiser as "the haves and the have-mores." But few GOP insiders ever attributed a mean spiritedness to the elder Bush. Indeed, he seemed to lack the sort of cocky nature that is attributed to his oldest son.

But here's the lowdown on the Bush family: there are two Bushes who understand public opinion and how it relates to politics, Barbara Bush and her son Jeb Bush.

George Bush the elder's political compass went awry once his feisty strategist and confidant Lee Atwater was diagnosed with cancer and died. Bush 41's term as president, much like that of his son's, seemed to soar when he declared war on Iraq. But his high popularity began to plummet as the impact of the housing and stock market slumps of the late 1980s combined with his decision to retract the promise he had asked voters in 1988 to read from his lips: "No new taxes." In a mind-blowing gaffe, Bush allowed Democratic leaders to bully him into breaking that promise, thus creating the biggest rift between Republicans and fiscally conservative independents that we had seen in many years.

This led conservative GOP political operative and onetime Nixon speechwriter Pat Buchanan to challenge Bush's reelection effort. Although the strength of a possible Buchanan challenge, particularly in the South, had already been anticipated by the

GOP, Buchanan shocked the Bush campaign with a stronger-than-expected showing in New Hampshire.

In 1992, Newt Gingrich was elected House Minority Whip, and House Minority Leader Bob Michel of Illinois decided to retire. (Newt had worn him down, I think.) Thus, Gingrich was assured of becoming, at a minimum, the minority leader after the 1994 elections. It fell upon our Gingrich political organization to help fight back the Buchanan movement in the South, this despite the fact that in some ways our policies were more like Buchanan's than President Bush's.

The problem was that we had to first get everyone—Gingrich, Bush, and a whole string of others—through the election year. And nothing was going right.

The first and most important moment in the 1992 election was what seemed to be a relatively inconsequential move to rearrange primary dates at the request of some Democratic leaders with whom we actually had very friendly behind-the-scenes relations. With concern over Bill Clinton's potential problems in the early Democratic contests of 1992, the Clinton forces, including their patron saint, Zell Miller, asked if Newt would support moving the Georgia GOP primary forward on the calendar to March 3, making it the first to follow New Hampshire.

Gingrich was the only Republican member of Georgia's Congressional delegation in 1992. After the Bush campaign determined that Buchanan didn't pose a threat to Bush in Georgia, the decision was made that Newt would send the message that he did not oppose moving the Georgia primary. I actually testified before a legislative committee on behalf of Gingrich and the GOP, the only purpose being to give the Bush Justice Department the Republican seal of approval for the move in dates. Georgia remained under the rules of the Voting Rights Act, and approval from Justice would be necessary. (In 2008, Republicans should have looked back on this strategic move when considering the move of the Florida and Michigan primaries.) Arguably, had we not given this move tacit GOP approval, Bill Clinton, who, as suspected, would find himself badly in need of a big win following more accusations from Gennifer Flowers, would have gone down the tubes.

Instead, Georgia became his turning point, and Zell Miller went on to proudly make the keynote address at the 1992 convention at Madison Square Garden, (As earlier noted, Miller has the distinction of being the only person to deliver a keynote address at both a Democratic and Republican National Convention.)

By the spring of 1992, it was obvious that President Bush was facing a political firestorm from many fronts. Buchanan was threatening to embarrass him in southern primaries, and Ross Perot, a Texas oil billionaire with a true axe to grind against Bush, was looking more and more like a viable third party-candidate.

The Bush re-election campaign was being managed by the late Robert Teeter. Teeter had been the pollster for the first U.S. Senate campaign in which I worked in 1980. He was one of the most accurate researchers/pollsters in America. But for some reason, his compass seemed a bit off in dealing with the Bush re-election. That may be because he was simply too nice a guy. And I don't think Bush would have made it through the South and survived Buchanan had Mary Matalin, a protégé of Atwater's, not asserted herself. She recognized critical details like the folly of sending President Bush to an Episcopal Church in a Southern Baptist town and reversed such decisions. She provided the fire and fight in the Bush 1992 campaign that was much needed in Atwater's absence.

But perhaps the biggest move made in the 1992 race came out of a meeting that was held after a Bush appearance at a large hotel in Atlanta. About ten or so of us met with President Bush after the speech and reiterated a suggestion that had been submitted to him before, but which he had ignored. We said he needed to apologize for moving his lips and raising taxes. He should say it had been wrong.

Unlike those true insiders who always have access to top leaders, I was usually present only for certain moments. This was one of those moments. Our message was blunt. In essence it was, "Mr. President, we don't think we are going to win back our base until we say the tax increase was a mistake."

Few in the group were close intimates of the president, and he looked at us as if we were Martians. Thankfully, President Bush was an open and very reasonable man. He took our blunt talk, and, rather than become defensive, he actively considered our message. Just days later, on the eve of the Georgia primary, Bush told the *Atlanta Journal-Constitution* that breaking his pledge not to raise taxes in his first term had been the "biggest blunder" of his presidency.

Our group may question whether it was our efforts that made the president offer his apology, but there was little doubt that the president's acknowledgment of his mistake blunted Buchanan's attacks in future contests for the nomination. In fact, I doubt President Bush 41 would have been able to mount much of a re-election effort at all without unifying his more conservative base with his "apology."

Nineteen ninety two was a wild political year. It was the year that the public seemed to rise up and say, "We are getting sick of the status quo." Incumbents on both sides of the aisle were under attack. We barely won Newt's own GOP primary that year in his congressional district reelection contest. And Ross Perot robbed Bush of critical voters who could have stuck with Bush had it been a two-man contest in that November's race.

Many years earlier, when I was just twenty years old and Gingrich was a minority-party freshman in Congress, he first told me that he would someday be Speaker of the House. Given the fact that, to that point in my life, I had never known a majority Republican House or Senate, I had to wonder if Newt was just ambitious or outrageously out of touch with reality.

And, as for the events that took place some twenty-four years later, I won't pretend that I was a centerpiece of Newt's successful Contract with America. Other, more gifted individuals played the critical roles in its active implementation in the 1994 season. In part, my involvement with what culminated in the Contract With America came years earlier as a youthful sounding board, along with other staffers and consultants who worked with Newt and a small band of then fresh-faced backbench Republican House members in creating what we then called the "Conservative Opportunity Society." As Newt noted later in his own writings, much of that earlier work served as the foundation of what would ultimately be the successful GOP platform in 1994.

By 1994 my primary mission was to see to it that Newt remained popular in his district, which had gone from being a nearly impossible one to win just two years earlier to a simple one in '94.

I didn't have to vie for Newt's attention, and he didn't have to coddle me like so many others who wanted a piece of his historic speakership. Frankly, I knew him well enough not to expect unending gratitude or an inextricably lifelong close relationship. It was simply not Newt's style, except in rare instances—and there is nothing rare about me. It is true that I paid him one of his first post-Speaker consulting "gigs" when we were starting our firm, but it was simple business and, to be kind, let me just say that he was charging prices that he likely learned to actually earn many years after his services with our firm came to an end!

But too many who have floated in and out of Newt Gingrich's life have left with only bitter words and unfair revisions of history. They suddenly recall new "dirty laundry" in his past. Let me say that most of the positive reforms in government our nation has seen since Ronald Reagan came during the first few years that Gingrich was Speaker of the House.

In my mind, Bill Clinton would never have seen such a boom in the economy had he not basically been forced to accept the Gingrich-led Republican effort to reduce the tax on capital gains. The resulting boom in the stock market and overall consumer confidence was phenomenal. While the rise of technology and Internet investments are credited with the economy of the late 1990s, most recognize that investment suddenly looked far more attractive and capital became more readily available as a result of the cuts.

Some of the Gingrich-led proposals, such as welfare reform, not only passed the House but made it into law. Regrettably, some of the strongest concepts, such as term limits for House and Senate members, passed the new GOP majority-controlled House in 1995 but failed to survive in the Senate.

There were times in implementing the Contract with America that the House leadership's success caused them to get ahead of public opinion. And, much more importantly, it seemed that they had no second act with which to follow the success they achieved in their early years of majority leadership.

All this led to the GOP congressional soldiers becoming restless. Newt now blames his leadership style—which he admits was still evolving at the time—for the problems the GOP encountered. But what's so odd is that there really weren't any major GOP screw-ups under Newt. Even with the so-called government shutdown, when Newt was labeled by news magazines as "The Gingrich Who Stole Christmas," and the Clinton impeachment effort that never gained traction with the public, Newt's Republican majority held even as his national approval ratings plummeted.

For decades, I had seen Newt concoct all sorts of vehicles for spreading whatever was his "newest new thing." Whether it was raising funds for his first book or inheriting the Republican political action committee known as GOPAC, we were always dodging bullets. Most, if not all, of the time, these bullets flew because Newt was, like most professors, two yards ahead of the rest of us. No one was there to dot all the I's or cross all the T's of his abstract dreams.

Moreover, Newt was a political figure the press loved to quote—and to hate. Long before he became speaker, things were so bad with the media that when Gingrich officially announced his move into a new, more upscale congressional district many miles away from the district he had represented, we decided that I would make the announcement and hand out a letter from Newt. The national press went nuts over his unwillingness to face them that day, but I remain convinced that had we done so, the thin margin by which we managed to win that race would never have materialized.

In 1997, the Democrats were able to pin ethics charges on Newt over his various failures to disclose information about one of his many brilliant but zany efforts to spread his ideas. To be clear, I was never a big enthusiast of these initiatives, such as GOPAC. Part of this was because, in my mind, such efforts created so many layers of distraction in Newt's life and so many fine lines to walk with regard to political and non-political use of dollars that the positives didn't outweigh the negatives. But I was looking at matters from a safe political view. Having not been gifted with Gingrich's intellect or vision, I could hardly see how an educational course on renewing America and changing civilization, broadcasted via satellite to locations around the nation, would really change anything.

And while I'm sure this, like so many of Newt's ideas, proved to be an additional brick in advancing his vision of America, it was not a happy moment waiting with Newt, attorneys Randy Evans and Ed Bethune, and former Senator Mack Mattingly in stone-cold silence as Newt prepared to go the floor of the House in 1997 to be sworn in to a second term. Gingrich had just dodged a coup among this Republican membership and was negotiating his way through what would be a reprimand from Congress citing him for failing to fully disclose information requested in a congressional investigation of his fundraising efforts related to what I had called "these whacky outside projects." I never took seriously the allegations that the use of non-profit dollars to fund things like Newt's "Renewing American Civilization" classes because, as I said, I saw no political upside and a huge downside to their mere existence. If Gingrich was guilty of anything, it was trying to take on too many complicated and involved projects that reached too few people and that had little, if any, political value. And by the way, the IRS never ruled that Gingrich violated any tax laws.

Even as he briefly considered a run for president in 2008, many observers expressed to me that Gingrich had too much baggage. That baggage included his past brushes with ethics issues and his numerous marriages. What? John McCain had been caught up in the Savings and Loan scandal many years earlier but, as is almost always the case, was really not the bad guy in the matter, as he was portrayed at the time. We had elected divorced candidates for president, including Ronald Reagan, and several of the top candidates on the Republican side in 2008 had admitted to inappropriate romantic relationships of some form or another.

I read accounts even today of Gingrich having been caught up in the 1992 congressional "check bouncing scandal," in which members were allegedly abusing the House of Representatives' bank by writing bad checks and failing to make good on them. Again they inaccurately state the real story. In a proactive move, I hired a team of accountants to reconstruct Newt's entire (and at that time less than significant) financial transactions. The truth is that it was the House bank that was failing to post deposits by most of the members of Congress who bounced checks. The accountants were able to establish that, had Gingrich's deposits been posted by the House bank when made, virtually none of his checks would have bounced. The same proved to be true for most House members—Republican and Democrat.

Perhaps the longest, weightiest piece of baggage for Gingrich was an urban legend passed down from a former aide, which said that Gingrich served his wife with divorce papers as she lay in her hospital bed recovering from cancer surgery. That was alleged to have happened in 1980, a time when I was constantly traveling with Gingrich. I know more details about his stops to phone booths to talk to his lawyer, to check on his daughters and their mother, than do many others. Let me disabuse everyone of this fabrication once and for all: The hospital smear as put forth above simply is not true.

Ironically, Newt's downfall came because in the 1998 election, the Republicans lost some ground but retained control of the House. By this time, GOP members of Congress had grown so spoiled and had so forgotten where they had been for decades before—in the minority—that they immediately started pointing fingers and attacking one another for their losses.

Gingrich's resignation in 1998 gets us to another of these moments in history that one can either call a moment of pure coincidence or conspiracy. And as usual, nothing can really be proved one way or another.

It is important to consider where the Republican Party might have found itself in 2008 had Newt Gingrich not resigned his position as speaker. By the time the 2000 presidential contest rolled around, the biggest name among conservative Republicans, Newt Gingrich, was gone. Had it not been for the relatively weak field of GOP candidates that George W. Bush faced that year, he might never have won the nomination.

In 1997 and 1998 Gingrich was quietly preparing for a possible run for the Republican nomination for president in 2000. If you find this funny, you're naïve. You have to remember that, although he had lost favor with independents and Democrats over his government shutdown maneuver, Gingrich remained popular with the conservative GOP base. These were the very voters he needed to carry critical early primary states such as Iowa, New Hampshire, and South Carolina. Gingrich had survived a 1997 coup attempt by a group of newer GOP House members, egged on, in my opinion, by the likes of then-House Majority Whip Tom "the Hammer" DeLay, plus other House Republican elders, all of whom chickened out and denied their roles after their plot failed.

Gingrich had used Bill Clinton as the perfect foil, much as Clinton had used Gingrich. The alleged acrimony which the public and press saw between the two was a Passion Play. Did anyone ever wonder why, if Clinton so disliked Gingrich, he would be willing to debate the Speaker of the House in New Hampshire as if the two were running for president against one another? And years later, why would Newt Gingrich declare over and over again that Hillary Clinton would win her party's nomination and could very well win the presidency? Has anyone ever questioned Hillary Clinton as to why she integrated parts of Gingrich's health transformation plan into her 2008 campaign stump speech?

The fact is that Newt Gingrich, the poster boy of an allegedly egg-headed and heartless conservative GOP, made Bill Clinton's polling numbers among independent voters soar. And Clinton's various alleged escapades and his exhortations against the Republican Congress served to lift Gingrich's profile among core conservative Republican voters in places like Iowa. (Iowa, by chance, was the home state of Gingrich's longtime and closest political advisor, D.C. operative Joe Gaylord, who over the years saw to it that Iowa Republican leaders got whatever they needed.)

Had Gingrich remained in Congress, held on to his role as Speaker of the House, and run for president in 2000, he would have overshadowed the other candidates with the star power of his position and a strong support base among conservatives. But Gingrich's decision to resign the speakership and his seat in Congress in November 1998 ended any hope of a presidential campaign. Ironically, it was the most powerful political leader in our nation at that time, a Democrat, who told me, in assessing the resignation, that, "it was DeLay who got him, Gingrich." Representative, now Senator, Lindsey Graham of South Carolina got the rap, along with some other alleged troublemakers, for pushing Newt out. But in subsequent conversations with former House members and others who had knowledge of the effort to push Gingrich aside, the name of the man they called "the Hammer" for his unrelenting determination to get what he wanted done, then-House Majority Whip DeLay, kept coming up as the "man behind the curtain," allegedly instructing and orchestrating pressure on Gingrich.

DeLay's dislike for Gingrich was well documented in his memoirs, in which DeLay had scathing words for the former speaker.

DeLay hardly enjoyed a close relationship with either George W. Bush or his political mastermind Karl Rove during Bush's years as governor of the same state of Texas that DeLay represented in Congress. Most describe the Bush approach to DeLay as one of extreme wariness, hardly the type of relationship that would foster the trust for collusion to eliminate a potential major presidential primary opponent.

But what's that saying, "Don't mess with Texas?" Once again, we have a likely coincidence that could be viewed as a conspiracy, one that helped to clear the field for what, in 1998, seemed the most unlikely of powerful contenders for the presidency. Newt Gingrich, *Time*'s "Person of the Year" just years earlier, had either fallen or been knocked off the political stage.

The era of George W. Bush would complete the creation of the "paranoid nation." His years in office would commence with the inheritance of a weakening economy and, within a year, an unprecedented attack of massive terror on the nation. What happened in the following years would set the stage for the longest and most contentious presidential election in modern history.

And as for Newt Gingrich, the man who was ignored and disliked by the first President Bush and replaced as the face of the GOP by the second Bush to hold the White House—he would return to haunt the family again. It would be, as John Feehery stated, "déjà vu all over again."

PART THREE

PARANOID PARTY

★ 16 ★

THE DECLINE AND FALL
OF THE GOP I KNEW

The 2008 political season would have been a year to remember simply because of the high stakes of the presidential election.

But aside from the gender, racial, and age issues on the surface, there was an underlying and overwhelming subplot—nothing less than the total disintegration of the Republican Party following its nearly three decades of domination in Congress or the White House.

In the early years, starting in 1980, the Republican Party often lived up to its governing philosophy, whether you think that's good or bad. But as the Contract with America receded from memory, the party began to lose its way.

For starters, let's set the stage for the plummet of George W. Bush from record-high approval ratings at the start of the wars in Iraq and Afghanistan to the pitiful final years of his second term.

By the time the 2008 election season was in high gear, many conservative and moderate Republicans and independents who voted for George W. Bush were in an uproar over the failures of eight years of the Bush administration, in which the White House fumbled away its clout, and during which the House of Representatives passed on countless opportunities to adhere to the Reagan philosophy of government.

There was huge spending. There was a large expansion of the Department of Education, which the Republicans had once vowed to eliminate. There was no concerted effort to back the chronic lip service of Republicans to overhaul the tax code. Immigration laws were a sick joke. The GOP leadership looked inept to even its most faithful followers.

Until I swore off active party politics in 1998 to write my book, and later a Creators Syndicate column and co-found a polling and political electronic news firm, I had been involved with the Republican Party at its highest levels for decades. Readers of my column know that I frequently voiced my concerns and that my nonpartisanship has never kept me from looking at the Republican Party, the one that gave us Ronald Reagan and took over the U.S. House in the 1994 elections, and asking, "Who stole my party?"

At one time, the GOP was the party that fought for open government, term limits, reductions in spending, and less government intrusion. When I had been involved in the Republican Party, we wanted the IRS disbanded and the Department of Education reduced, made useful, or abolished. We believed in the inherent goodness of the individual and the greatness of individualism.

Then, after the Republicans took the White House and then the House and the Senate, it was just all too tempting to become the establishment that most Republicans had railed against for years. I could name you plenty of members of Congress who promised term limits. Most are either still there, were defeated, or just couldn't avoid the lure of making big money, by lobbying and such, while their colleagues were still in power. Greed ruined the GOP I loved. Suddenly everybody decided that they could carry on their magic and turn a quick buck.

As far as reducing government, the GOP had helped create endless additional laws and spent wild amounts of money in the same manner as the Democrats we used to criticize. It took the so-called neoconservative economists, those insulated prigs, months and months to figure out that there was a housing finance crisis. That's because in D.C., the local economy was thriving because of its proximity to power and wealth.

Republicans had a lousy cast of leading candidates in 2008. The two early front-runners were a guy, Mitt Romney, who looked slicker than a television preacher, and another, Mike Huckabee, who really was a preacher but couldn't seem to decide how to run a campaign. It was a mess. It's just that simple. (Not that the Democrats had anything to brag about, but that's their problem.)

Just think: these candidates spent half their time talking about the issue of immigration in a state, Iowa, where there is no immigration problem. On the flip side, the candidates held that debate on CNN in November in St. Petersburg, Florida, and never once mentioned the housing crisis there, in the state that had seen been the biggest drop in home values in the nation.

Why was this lot running for president? What were their ideas to get the nation's economy moving? Who was willing to shake up our ludicrous system of taxation? How would we actually stop wasting endless tax dollars on "bridges to nowhere?"

Most Americans don't want to regulate people's lives. We don't want to regulate the lives of everyone in every other nation of the world. The truth is, most of us don't feel like paying for everyone else's problems while we still see kids dropping out of school and homeless veterans roaming our city streets.

No matter what leaders emerged for either party, many of us feared that we seemed to be headed for four more years of nothing.

★ 17 ★

THAT WAR THING

Aside from general frustration and concern about the dominant geopolitical issue of the Bush administration, many Americans were simply puzzled about the run-up to war in Iraq in 2002. The country wanted to know if Iraq really was a true crisis. If so, why the senseless effort at building an international coalition, one that, in the end, might never develop or prove to hold much political water?

In the plea for international approval of U.S. war actions, the politicians and diplomats should have remembered that so-called international coalitions—from the nineteenth-century First Concert of Europe, whose collapse led to the Crimean War, to the United States' current uneasy relationship with other Western nations—almost never prove to be sources of significant geopolitical stability.

What people in places like Missouri, Texas, Michigan, and elsewhere throughout the heartland were really interested in (other than whether they would be able to hold onto their jobs, get a raise, or possibly witness the resurrections of their 401(k)s) was getting the best information about the commander-in-chief's rationale and plan for the execution of the war in Iraq.

Americans understood that Saddam Hussein was a bad guy, and many thought that Bush 41 should have dispatched him ten years ago. But the current administration, the American people felt, was being sucked into a ring-around-the-rosy battle over diplomacy vs. action.

Rather than attempting to build a coalition of half-hearted Western nations, President Bush should have spoken to his own citizens by means of the time-tested and successful nine-o'clock televised address to the nation, the sort of "this-is-important-stuff" speech that left most Americans stunned back during the Cuban Missile Crisis of 1962. The backdrop, the Oval Office, for some reason avoided by Bush.

This was a crisis, wasn't it?

In such a speech, the president should have unveiled incontrovertible evidence of Iraq's acceleration of its development of a nuclear weapons program, as well as an arsenal of chemical and biological weapons, much as the Kennedy administration produced similarly incriminating evidence against the Soviet Union's stockpile of weapons in Cuba.

After all, we did have such evidence, didn't we?

Then the president should have explained the various international resolutions, past precedents, and Constitutional precepts that allowed him the legal and moral standing to take immediate action to meet pressing circumstances and protect the safety of the United States and the stability of the world.

This was a circumstance calling for immediate action, wasn't it?

After reminding the nation, and more importantly, the world, that Saddam Hussein had steadfastly refused to cooperate with arms-control inspectors, Bush should have proceeded to announce that the United States had initiated a military operation to finally topple Saddam's regime and liberate the people of Iraq.

The Democrats howled, the Western allies bellyached, and our "Arab coalition" denounced our actions. But in short order, Saddam joined the ranks of totalitarian tinhorn dictators like Moammar Qadhafi and Manuel Noriega, never to be feared again.

The vast majority of Americans were initially supportive and thankful. Supportive because they were tired of reading and hearing about this madman Hussein, who had been allowed to go virtually unchecked over the previous decade, thankful because they weren't dragged through week after week of hand-wringing and second-guessing during silly congressional hearings and "shuttle diplomacy." Americans know instinctively that all the pointless debate over whether or not to go to war always serves mainly to make it tougher for the economy to stabilize and therefore tougher to provide them and their wallets with some measure of protection.

It wasn't that voters in Ohio or Florida or Alaska were less sophisticated than those who endlessly analyzed our options against Saddam. It was really more a matter of common sense. Average Americans found it difficult to understand why we had to waste time pleading our case before the United Nations or taking a moral tongue-lashing from the Germans, the French, or even the Canadians, when our own president and his leaders kept arguing that Iraq posed a real and current danger.

It was a real and present danger, wasn't it?

John Kennedy faced a rapid ramp-up in Cuba's ability to launch what were the most dangerous weapons of mass destruction of the era. It was a matter of days, not months, before JFK responded with authority to prevent the construction of potentially deadly ballistic weapons near the U.S. coastline.

If Saddam really was the threat that Bush and his intelligence advisors believed him to be, the president should have taken heart that most who live outside of the Beltway wouldn't fret over whether the United Nations approved of his actions or whether the French would issue another of their "stinging rebukes" over U.S. policy.

If Iraq was an imminent threat, the president should have gotten to it. He shouldn't have let the detractors allow the issue to linger so that the economy suffered further and the Democrats started taking advantage of the situation while his administration pleaded its case in a series of venues where approval was far too little and far too late. The American people care about what is relevant to preserving their personal and economic security, not what diplomats and politicians have to say.

Those questions and concerns from before the war still lingered in the minds of many Americans as the race for the presidency in 2008 played out. They wanted to support the troops, and did, but they were still wondering about the exact reasons for launching the war. "We did have evidence of weapons of mass destruction, didn't we?" "There was no recourse other than invasion, right?" "Iraq did pose a tangible danger to America, right?" These questions would haunt the Bush White House and would remain a part of political discourse for years to come. The problem for Bush was that he never used the definitive approach of the national televised address to rally the American people. He failed to make symbolic use of the Oval Office to focus national attention on the war. That would have sent the proper message to the nation that Iraq was of the utmost importance.

Just as he never made a definitive case for the war, Bush was less than resolute in declaring the success of the surge of military troops which, according to several reports, he was the minority, even among his own military advisers, in supporting. As the 2008 election headed towards its last months, the war in Iraq remained controversial. But even Democrats were having increased difficulty in saying that the surge of troops Bush sent to the region in 2007 and 2008 had been anything but a success.

★ 18 ★

IGNORING EARLY SIGNS
OF PROBLEMS TO COME

Early into his administration, before the war and well before his reelection, many wondered if the Bush administration was ignoring issues that would haunt it down the road. Although the unhappy repercussions of Bush's inattention to key developments wouldn't be felt until after his reelection in 2004, the warning signs were there years before.

At least as early as 2002, conventional wisdom would have suggested that the president was taking the right political course in concentrating on foreign policy. He doubtless remembered that it was Bush 41's domestic agenda that caused his father's fall from lofty polling numbers just a year after the victory in the Persian Gulf War. The elder Bush had been hoodwinked by Democrats—and some Republicans—into backing a tax increase despite his 1988 campaign declaration of "Read my lips: No new taxes."

George W. was being properly advised by Karl Rove not to ignore domestic issues even while he was succeeding brilliantly in dealing with the attack on America launched on September 11, 2001. And Bush had begun this effort by saying that a tax increase would take place "over [his] dead body." Those were strong words, backed by a strong push to pass the GOP economic stimulus plan comprised of tax cuts.

So where was the fault in Bush's strategy? After all, every political pro knows that pocketbook issues are the ultimate determining factor in almost any election. Nevertheless, there were significant issues on the horizon that Republicans should have recognized would be of greater importance to them in key states. These states could well have tipped the delicate balance of control of the House of Representatives following the 2002 election, and over the course of the next four years, that balance would indeed shift. Democratic Senate Majority Leader Tom Daschle quietly formulated an interesting scenario that linked together seemingly unrelated issues into a unique political assault, including energy conservation, availability of water resources, and securities fraud.

The Democratic strategy began with strong criticism of Vice President Dick Cheney's offhand suggestion early in the Bush administration that energy conservation would not be a high policy priority. This led to some quick cleanup work by Bush, who quelled criticism of the vice president by saying that America couldn't conserve its way to energy independence. But Cheney's remark gave the Democrats political traction to question the Bush administration's cozy relationship with some oil and other energy producers, including the formerly high-flying, now bankrupt, Enron Corp.

The Democrats believed that it was a Bush-team blunder for the president and his advisers to myopically concentrate on the issues of tax reform and education. They knew the dirty little secret that few political experts ever want to admit—unless you are handing out scholarship checks, exit polls consistently show that while voters always rate education reform as a top issue, they almost never let it decide how they will vote. And while pocketbook issues are almost always the key to an election victory, it was unclear whether the next round of proposed GOP tax cuts would capture the average voter's heart by the time the November elections rolled around.

The Democrats were also convinced that U.S. dependence on the unstable Middle East for oil, coupled with the scandal that surrounded the Enron collapse, would ultimately be the issue that would hit closer to home that fall. The Democrats asked questions about the administration's true commitment to energy alternatives, alternatives they suggested could protect us from energy dependence on hostile countries and shore up our shaky national security, and that would have prevented the current pain at the gas pump.

Added to the issue of oil dependence was that of other precious natural resources. For example, the Colorado River now often dries up before reaching the Gulf of California. Many states faced increasing water restrictions and a bleak future for water supplies. In some big states, such as Florida, water was near the top of voters' lists of concerns.

All of these energy and resource problems were overlaid with scandal. Consider the fall-out from the Enron situation, which played a part in Republican losses down the road. A prime example of the administration's tone deafness came from Securities and Exchange Commission Chairman Harvey Pitt, who was quoted in *Barron's* as saying that there was no immediate need to change the reporting procedures for publicly traded companies. That despite the fact that Enron's public filings just the year before its failure gave little indication to its investors and employees that a financial collapse was looming.

Although a little battered, the Bush administration survived the corporate integrity scandal. But the White House sewed further seeds of destruction when it failed to put forth a comprehensive energy plan. That mistake started coming home to roost in the 2008 election season.

In a press conference held in early 2008, Bush was asked by a reporter about news that gas might reach four dollars a gallon. Bush appeared surprised, saying in essence that he had heard no such news. Only a few months later, many Americans were paying even more than that.

★ 19 ★

THE PROBLEM WITH CHENEY

Sometimes politicians' success with the public depends as much on good presentation as it does on good policy.

Following President Bush's tepid speech to the nation on September 7, 2003, in which he delivered the bad news that he would request an additional eighty-seven billion dollars for the reconstruction of Iraq, the president's declining approval ratings accelerated their downward slide. That prompted a rare television appearance by Vice President Dick Cheney on NBC's *Meet the Press* to help improve public perception.

Cheney had no trouble coming across as bright and confident on TV. But while conservative partisans rarely want to acknowledge the truth until it runs them over, it has to be said that Cheney's cool and polished brilliance could have the effect of unsettling many viewers.

Cheney's deliberate, understated style bordered on condescension. In answering what could fairly be termed a barrage of tough questions by host Tim Russert, the vice president brushed off the fact that no weapons of mass destruction had been discovered in Iraq with a glib answer suggesting that such weapons did exist, whether or not proof can be found.

When Russert confronted Cheney with his own quotes criticizing former President Reagan in the 1980s for excessive budget deficits, the vice president said that the nation has often made exceptions for unique circumstances like war. A reasonable answer, but one that might leave those of us who considered Reagan a great president wondering whether the threat from the Cold War of his era was not an equally compelling justification for accelerated deficit spending.

Russert went on to question Cheney about his and his staff members' frequent visit to CIA headquarters. At this point, even the strongest supporters of the administration could recognize that the vice president was a little too hands-on sure of himself.

And therein lies the problem. For while Cheney seemed almost eerily confident in the Bush White House's every move, much of the nation was unsure as to how and when the conflict in Iraq would end and at what cost in blood and treasure. Compound that insecurity with an equally strong lack of public understanding of the reasons for the nation's economic troubles and confidence in Bush's competence to deal with them, and it's easy to see why the administration needed to review not only its policies with increased scrutiny, but also its manner of publically presenting those policies.

Cheney's sheer command of the issues appeared to overshadow those of the president. But understanding policy does not always translate into an impression that one comprehends political reality. And the reality is that a number of moderates and conservatives who supported both the war in Iraq and the president's domestic agenda had long wanted a clearer picture of where we are headed. What would be the final cost of the wars in Iraq and Afghanistan? Was there a policy in the works to address employment issues, the increase in home foreclosures, and the failure of major financial institutions? And how will we deal with deficits far in excess of those in the Reagan years?

The vice president and others who spoke for the president needed to connect more with the public by acknowledging reality and by presenting a clearer plan for dealing with it.

★ 20 ★

NOT JUST A REPUBLICAN
MELTDOWN

Just a few months into the 2004 campaign season, it was clear that both political parties were already headed in the wrong direction on key issues. Both Congress and the White House, overwhelmed with the paranoia of a reelection campaign, were collectively chasing their own tails. Here are just two examples of how out-of-touch and silly the two major parties' presidential campaigns had already become by February of that year.

First, the Democrats. For the first week or so of the month, party leaders had fueled constant debate about whether President Bush fulfilled his military obligation to the Texas Air National Guard in the early 1970s. The White House had been forced to release all types of records and even produce a former officer who said that Bush was present and accounted for.

The truth is that no one but hard-core political insiders cared one way or the other. We all knew that John Kerry was a war hero and expected that he would lord that fact over Bush during the fall campaign. But instead of modestly reminding voters of their candidate's Vietnam heroics at the appropriate times, the Democrats were determined to pound their chests and belittle Bush's own military service. They were barking up the wrong tree. For all of his alleged or actual weaknesses as president, Bush continued to be viewed as a brave commander-in-chief who stood up to terrorists and international despots, often with little or no support from other nations.

In endlessly stoking the flames of the mismatch in Kerry's and Bush's Vietnam War-era military experience, the media and the Democrats started to make Bush look worthy of sympathy, something that had once seemed impossible. Bush, who has always irritated some conservative voters with what they deem a cocky swagger, appeared to be the victim of a petty campaign dredged up by nitpickers willing to do anything to make the commander-in-chief look like the one thing he clearly wasn't, a coward.

Now, the Republicans. On January 20, 2004, Bush left many of us scratching our heads as we listened to his State of the Union address. Among the other weighty topics he touched on—the budget, health care, the war in Iraq, terrorism—why did he insert rhetoric about subjects that were totally out of place in a speech so momentous, such as his "call on team owners, union representatives, coaches, and players to take the lead, to send the right signal, to get tough, and to get rid of steroids now?"

The answer came some weeks later, when Attorney General John Ashcroft appeared in a press conference to announce a major Federal bust of distributors of steroids to big-name professional athletes. What a shock! About as shocking as discovering cork in a bat or grease on a baseball. A problem, maybe. An issue rigged for the president, definitely.

It should be up to the various professional sports leagues to regulate and police the use of performance-enhancing drugs. But when jobs are hemorrhaging out of the United States and a little old lady can't board an airplane without being stripped to her underwear, steroid use is a top concern of the White House? How could our elected officials be so out of touch?

Most Americans don't have the time or interest to play private investigator on what the president did when he was young. Nor do they want their law enforcement agencies making steroid use a higher priority than young Americans dying overseas and unidentified snipers shooting at cars in Ohio.

I've said it before, and I'll say it again: both major political parties get these silly strategic ideas from insulated policy wonks who spend their time conferring with one another in an echo chamber instead of taking the public's pulse.

★ 21 ★

A FAILURE TO LEAD

Perhaps one of the few bold and innovative Reagan-esque ideas to come along during the Bush years was a proposal championed by a senior member of Congress and popularized by a syndicated radio talk-show host. Republican U.S. Representative John Linder and the self-described High Priest of the Church of the Painful Truth, talk radio's Neal Boortz, published The *FairTax Book: Saying Goodbye to the Income Tax and the IRS* in 2005 and the book stormed its way to the top of the *New York Times* bestseller list.

Understanding the FairTax takes an open mind. While the FairTax would eliminate the federal income tax and the Internal Revenue Service along with it, it would establish a national sales tax on retail consumption. It would eliminate the current crazy quilt of indecipherable tax code regulations that bogs down businesses and befuddles families. It would make each of us the master of our own financial destinies.

If you wanted to spend your money, that road would be wide open to you with the FairTax. If you wanted to save instead, you wouldn't be penalized for having rightfully earned your money in the first place.

Past polling has suggested that, when properly explained, the FairTax proposal, which would end the Federal government's fixation on punishing those who work hard, is extremely popular. But tell that to Linder, the man who has championed the idea in recent years.

Linder, who began his stint in Congress in 1993, is a dentist by training, a successful businessman in his past career, and as bright a public servant as one would ever hope to meet. But in Washington, like everywhere else, there are certain circles of power, certain styles which are expected, and a huge aversion to rocking boats unless such rocking is really a gentle push or the public wants the boat to be taken to the depths of the deep blue sea.

But being smart and devoted to a cause rarely gets rewarded in the nation's capital. For years, Linder tried in vain to get the Bush White House and top congressional leaders to seriously consider his most logical proposal.

Pushing for complete overhaul of something as broken as our current income tax system when the overhaul doesn't benefit some major source of political power in Washington is never viewed as smart politics. So rather than fight for an end of a form of taxation that results in putting a burden on initiative and risk, requires a bloated bureaucracy to enforce its intricacies, and supports a world of big accounting and law firms, the real legislative push in 2004 was for the so-called privatization of Social Security.

Now that's something that should have sprouted wings, right? After all, allowing taxpayers to put some cash away in private funds might just have given a big boost to those who handle investments. Not that I'm opposed to the concept. But with a thousand questions out there about the proposal's cost and workability, this proposal seems far more radical and risky than the life-altering taxation change proposed by Linder.

In 2006, a Congressman who was just another freshman during the Republican Revolution of the 1990s lamented the fact that people back in his Tennessee district seemed more interested in things like a bestselling book promoting the FairTax than in changing Washington.

The statement from Representative Zach Wamp has always distilled for me just how far many Republican members of Congress really are from their constituents in terms of priorities and, more importantly, reality. Let's take a trip down memory lane and recount an idea that Wamp and many of his colleagues were touting—back when they were the bright-eyed candidates of reform.

Way back in 1994, many of our Republican candidates were attacking a corrupt Congress made up of entrenched, pork-spending Democratic leaders who, in many cases, had held their seats for decades and were out of touch with the American people.

The reformers pointed to the questionable dealings of former Speaker of the House Jim Wright, who was essentially run out of office as a result of an inquiry by the House Ethics Committee, and the strong-arm tactics of the top Democratic leaders in the House. Sound familiar?

The fact is, Wamp and his colleagues, who shocked the nation by taking control of the House in the 1994 elections, delivered a strong conservative agenda and even put rules into effect that limited the number of years a member could serve as chairman of a committee. In fact, many of those eager new reformists declared that they would adhere to their own self-imposed term limits. Wamp was one of those who made such a declaration, pledging to serve absolutely no more than six two-year terms.

By 2008, Wamp was comfortably entrenched in his seventh term. How could this be? Wamp has a simple explanation. In an April 2006 interview in *USA Today*, Wamp declared that he had made a mistake in pledging to limit his service in Congress to a mere twelve years.

Unlike many of his colleagues, Wamp got lucky in the 2006 elections. Many of his colleagues also failed to recognize that the

GOP was in serious danger of losing control of Congress in the 2006 election if they didn't start moving with lightning speed in addressing the impatience of their own base. Public opinion surveys showed that people (even many Republicans) wanted viciously tough ethics reform, and that the backlash toward those once bright-eyed freshmen was starting to create a movement to throw the bums out. To his credit, Wamp later moved to supporting the Fair Tax.

But, the permanent Republican majority that Newt and others—including yours truly—worked for fourteen years to secure was gone.

★ 22 ★

THE TRUE START OF GOP DECLINE:
THE SCHIAVO INTERVENTION

In the midst of the complacency and inaction of the GOP on issues of true concern to the American people, there came two events that collectively sealed the fate of not only the GOP, but of President Bush.

The first was the decision on the part of the Bush administration and Congress to get in the middle of a battle between family members over pulling the plug on the life-sustaining medical equipment of a brain-damaged woman, Terri Schiavo.

I personally had strong reservations about Schiavo's husband's claim that she once told him never to sustain her life with the use of medical machinery. I was particularly uneasy with that claim, given that he had spent the last ten years of his wife's vegetative state living with another woman and even fathering two children by her.

As a casual observer of the Schiavo situation, I gave the benefit of the doubt to the suffering parents who wanted to keep their daughter alive by any means necessary. We should all believe that miracles can and do happen. Some media have drawn a picture of Schiavo's husband as the biggest victim besides Terri herself. To me, he doesn't invite such a sympathetic portrait.

But my personal beliefs about this sad case diverge from the sentiments of the majority of the American people. As a pollster, I can tell you that the popularity of the GOP-led Senate and House began to drop immediately after the decision to override the State of Florida on the Schiavo matter and intervene from Washington. Don't get me wrong. I was rooting for Congress to do what it had to do in order to get Terri Schiavo back on her feeding tube.

Few recall that in the 1992 presidential primary, President George H. W. Bush was drifting into the camps of the vocal abortion opponents and the so-called Christian Coalition. This was partly a function of his eight years as vice president to Ronald Reagan. But it was also a result of having to face Pat Robertson in the Republican primaries of 1988 and then a surprisingly strong Pat Buchanan in 1992.

After Bush's defeat in 1992, otherwise strong conservative Republicans started drifting away from the anti-abortion movement. Media interviews at the time showed that many of these one-time social-conservative candidates and elected officials were starting to temper their positions on social issues. Many were saying off-the-record that the GOP should stick to a message of fiscal and governmental restraint and lessen its efforts to legislate morality.

This was an overreaction. It was caused partly by the failure of many Republicans to recognize that President Bush's defeat had been as much a result of the spoiler effect of third-party candidate Ross Perot as it had been because of any rebellion by the Republican base of the religious right.

In 2005, pundits from both the Republican and Democratic sides had come to believe that activist government interventions on behalf of anything appealing to the conservative religious voting bloc would be politically significant.

All of this is well and good except for one thing. The public mood is changeable. Public opinion polls on the Schiavo matter consistently showed that most Americans believed that her feeding tube should have been removed. Admittedly, few have more than a limited knowledge of Schiavo's circumstances. Nevertheless, the polling numbers were strong and flew in the face of the conventional wisdom of many political experts.

Congress interjecting itself into a state court case at the eleventh hour and passing emergency legislation offering one person access to the federal court, contrary to long-standing patterns, set a troubling precedent. It would severely weaken future congressional efforts to respect principles of federalism and separation of powers.

Over the past few years since the Schiavo case, Republican legislators and Congress appeared to be running contrary to perhaps the most important precept of the GOP and conservative movements. We have seen ever more intervening, regulating, and imposing of new policies at every turn.

Much of the impulse arises from the necessary reaction to the attacks of September 11, 2001, or as a response to Enron and similar corporate scandals. Still, Republican legislators and lawmakers needed to step back and closely examine whether many of these actions were truly rooted in the philosophy of less government and more personal responsibility, or whether they are in fact sops to special interest groups and narrow (but activist) voting blocs whose electoral clout could eventually fade. Whatever the reason or justification, it seems that practically every day brought the nation new requirements, rules, regulations, and programs that further complicate and invade our private lives.

Republicans needed to keep in mind that the public's mood could turn. Americans would wake up one day and suddenly say they've had enough of what once seemed to be a good thing.

★ 23 ★

THE CRUSHING BLOW:
HURRICANE KATRINA

If the complacency of the GOP House wasn't enough to start a catastrophic slide for the Republicans, Hurricane Katrina came close to sealing the deal. The Federal Emergency Management Agency's bungled response to the storm guaranteed that the Republicans, and in particular Bush, would see their public approval ratings go into freefall.

It's true that the Bush White House was slow to react to the storm that flooded much of New Orleans and the Gulf Coast and created one of the most significant and longest-lasting natural disasters in our nation's history. But the national media also deserved a bit of the blame.

As fate would have it, InsiderAdvantage, the company that I lead, purchased the long-established, Washington, D.C.-based Southern Political Report in the same week that Hurricane Katrina struck New Orleans. As the storm approached land we were in the last stages of creating a daily web-based version of the publication. Immediately, we called on all the resources of the SPR, including its vast network of contacts, many of whom lived in Katrina's path.

As early as Monday afternoon, we realized that the Category 4 storm was far more devastating than was being reported by the

TV news networks. For starters, our sources said that New Orleans would start to flood by daybreak Tuesday. They also explained how entire foundations of the coastal economy, such as the burgeoning casino resorts along the Mississippi River, had been erased. By late Tuesday night, we had been told off-the-record that the commonly reported death toll of about eighty would likely swell into the thousands in the days to come.

So why, on Tuesday night, was network television airing shows like *Tommy Lee Goes to College*, instead of providing 24/7 live coverage of this historic, catastrophic event? Where were the rock stars announcing soon-to-come mega-concerts to raise quick cash for the stricken region? And why in the world was the stock market rising on both Monday and Wednesday?

This isn't to knock the courageous and resourceful print, broadcast, and online reporters on the scene or the media venues that devoted practically all their column space or airtime to this cataclysmic event. I'm aiming higher with my complaint, at the top-level program directors and network executives who think that earthquakes in California and attacks on New York warrant the full attention of the world, but life-threatening emergencies in the swamps and backwoods of the South or in the Midwest don't.

Nevertheless, the intolerably slow, bulky reaction to the disaster by the Bush administration was unbelievable. The White House even blamed the underreporting of the hurricane's damage in early reports by media for FEMA's foot-dragging.

I blame those working for the president. Federal Emergency Management Agency Director Michael Brown, who came to the disaster-response division of the Department of Homeland Security after multiple lawsuits forced him to resign as the Judges and Stewards Commissioner of the International Arabian Horse Association, simply was not up to the task.

The Republicans who defended the pitiful early response to Katrina—or the lack of it—did the president and the GOP a disservice by making the party appear out of touch. The irony of President Bush's congratulatory statement to Brown—"Brownie, you're doing a heck of a job!"—could not have been more acute.

But Democrats had their own losers in all of this. One was the governor of Louisiana, Kathleen Blanco. She was probably the weakest leader in a crisis I've ever seen. She should have enrolled in the Jeb Bush School of Effective Hurricane Response. For my money, the former Florida governor remains a model of active yet measured response to the devastation brought by these storms.

Perhaps President Bush would have done well to turn management of Katrina over to his younger brother Jeb. Regardless, the situation remained a black eye. Whole areas around New Orleans were still rotting in 2008. And scores of temporary housing trailers, which arrived long after the survivors had scattered to the four corners of the nation, sat in fields, their walls having collapsed or having been discovered to emit dangerous levels of toxic gases. One by one the forced lines of temporary pre-fab houses began to fold one on top of another like the collapsing house of cards that was becoming the Republican legacy of the decade.

PART FOUR

PARANOID CAUCUS

★ 24 ★

IOWA AND THE
DES MOINES REGISTER EFFECT

Can a single poll change the direction of a major political race? You bet. If you don't believe it, just follow the story of the *Des Moines Register*'s poll early in the 2008 presidential contest.

Years ago, when our company first started polling public opinion and political races, an editor at a medium-sized newspaper told me—much to my chagrin—that he didn't like running political polls because he felt they influenced the voters too much. At the time I thought, "what an out-of-touch guy—polls are a staple of newspapers and political coverage." I still believe I was right. But then again, he might have been onto something, too.

The particular city where this editor then reigned is about the same size and has about the same national name recognition as does Des Moines, Iowa. And the two cities and their respective newspapers have something else in common. Unlike many cities in America, these two do not suffer from the problem of having a major daily with a news and editorial bent that is out of step with its peoples' majority political philosophy.

Iowa remains a relatively small moderate-to-conservative state where people treat one another with that small-town respect that so much of America has lost. The state certainly has its share of Democrats, and even liberal Democrats, as was made clear the day after the 2008 Iowa caucus. But regardless of party affiliation, most Iowans feel that the *Des Moines Register* is fair, balanced, and reliable. And because Iowa doesn't have many "big city" dailies, the *Register* is the only game, not only in town, but also in the state as a whole.

Since its appearance in 1943 as the first national newspaper political poll, the Iowa Poll has gained the reputation of being the gold standard for polling of the presidential caucuses, especially when the race is a competitive one. In 2004 it was a *Des Moines Register* poll that was able to sort through a seeming three-way race in which former Vermont Governor Howard Dean was dropping, and Senators John Edwards of North Carolina and John Kerry of Massachusetts were battling to take the lead. The *Des Moines Register* poll declared just days before the election that Kerry was ahead and, voilà, he won the Iowa Democratic Caucus a few days later and went on to win his party's nomination.

Fast forward to the phenomenally wild Iowa contest of 2008. When the State of Florida maneuvered to set its primary ahead of most others, Iowa, New Hampshire, and South Carolina countered by moving their contests forward on the calendar to remain the first major contests of the presidential season.

Iowa's would prove to be the backbreaker. Scheduled for January 3, the caucuses would require both the Democratic and Republican candidates to forgo celebrating the Christmas and New Year holidays and vie for the attention of Iowans, many of whom would be in holiday mode up until the day before the caucuses were held.

The timing of the caucuses made polling the race a nightmare, as well. How do you know if people are home or interested in politics during the long and busy holiday season? Well, none of us in the business were really sure. But in hindsight, it was very clear that Iowans are uniquely qualified to keep politics on the brain throughout the holidays. Because of the size of the state and limited air travel, Iowa does not see the mass exodus of residents that, say, a New York or even a North Carolina might encounter during the holidays. It seemed to those of us covering the races and polling them that the opposite was true. It seemed that every Iowan who could vote stayed right by their television set watching campaign ads, or attended political rallies, or just plain waited in their homes to turn out in record numbers for both the Republican and Democratic contests.

A review of the political polls taken in December, as the race approached the January 3 caucus, showed a clear pattern of Hillary Clinton leading the Democratic pack. In fact, in the weeks leading up to the release of the *Des Moines Register* poll, not a single major national poll, including polls by the *Los Angeles Times*, CNN, Zogby, Rasmussen, and our firm, InsiderAdvantage, showed Barack Obama leading in Iowa. The Mason-Dixon/MSNBC poll showed former Senator John Edwards leading.

That was interesting because, just as it had in the 2004 race, our InsiderAdvantage poll did something that the other polls did not. What we did gave credence to the Mason-Dixon/MSNBC poll and helps explain just how powerful the *Des Moines Register* poll turned out to be in creating a self-fulfilling prophesy for a Barack Obama win in Iowa. I found the Mason-Dixon results quite telling because that firm specializes in rural and Southern states and tends to pick up trends in those areas that many other pollsters often miss.

Because of the nature of the Democratic caucus in Iowa, it is my belief that it is essential that pollsters ask those being polled not only whom they intend to vote for, but also who their second choice would be. This is because of the Iowa Democratic Party rule that, if the candidate one supports at one's local caucus fails to receive at least fifteen percent of the vote at that caucus location, then one must realign and cast a vote for one of the remaining candidates who received the required fifteen percent or more of the vote; or else, they can simply choose not to vote.

If Mason-Dixon and our firm were correct, Iowa's Democratic contest would be a tight finish. In fact, every poll suggested a three-way battle between Clinton, Obama, and Edwards. That is, until the "golden one" appeared.

★ 25 ★

INFLUENTIAL GOLD

For whatever reason, our opinion research firm is one of the few polling operations that includes the critically important second-choice question in our Iowa polling. In 2004 the *Des Moines Register* released its supposed "gold standard" poll just days before the vote. The Iowa Poll showed Senator John Kerry suddenly bursting ahead of the energized Governor Howard Dean, the generally popular former Representative Dick Gephardt of Missouri, and Senator John Edwards. We followed up with our poll, asking respondents both their first and second choices. We then reallocated the numbers to reflect who, in the poll, was not at the required fifteen percent level and to whom the "second-choice" votes would go. It resulted in our firm providing the clearest and most accurate look at how Iowa actually stacked up in 2004.

It's critical that I explain the methodology and accuracy of our unique and practical approach to polling Iowa in 2004 before I make the rather controversial case that the respected *Des Moines Register* poll was, in 2008, not only potentially methodologically flawed and prone to produce bad results, but had an actual impact in changing the minds of caucus attendees just before the Democratic caucus was to begin.

During the 2004 Democratic battle for the nomination, columnist Robert Novak, in a January 19, 2004, column, took note of our effort to poll the second choice of those voters whose candidates were not going to make the cut. That poll showed that, contrary to what most thought, there was no three-way race between Howard Dean, John Kerry, and Richard Gephardt. We pegged it as a solid Kerry lead.

After that historical bolstering of our methodology, let me take a step back and say that there were some organizations that did, in the 2008 Democratic battle, poll the second choice of potential caucus participants and reallocated just as we had done for those votes. the *Washington Post*/ABC News survey of Iowa voters in December 2007 did just that and found Obama receiving more of the votes of those who, if their first candidate of choice did not meet the minimal level of support required, would have to choose a new candidate.

The *Post*/ABC poll took place in mid-December, but the next poll to be released in Iowa was a December poll by our firm. It also showed Obama in the lead. Ironically, as Clinton and Edwards seemed to surge, the RealClearPolitics (the "gold standard" web site that publishes all major political polls in the nation) compilation of surveys in Iowa never showed Obama in the lead again until after the release of the *Des Moines Register* poll.

Now let me explain why I believe that the *Des Moines Register* poll was way off in where the race truly was when it was released just three days before the caucus was to take place and how much the poll's definitive Obama lead influenced the actual vote in the Iowa Democratic caucus.

In the weeks heading up to the Iowa caucus, John Edwards appeared to be strong and getting stronger, if not already the leader in the race. If he wasn't the leader in the race, then, as the Mason-Dixon poll showed it, he was at least an increasingly popular second-place choice.

Our one InsiderAdvantage poll taken before the *Des Moines Register* poll showed, using our first- and second-choice methodology, Clinton leading with thirty percent, Edwards at twenty-nine percent, and Obama at twenty-two percent. The Zogby poll had Clinton at thirty percent, with Obama and Edwards tied at twenty–six percent. And, as I mentioned earlier, the Mason-Dixon/MSNBC poll showed Edwards ahead.

In the last week or so before the Iowa Democratic caucus, I was receiving reports from volunteers and staff in the Edwards campaign confirming that their own polling numbers showed the populist former North Carolina senator gaining ground and showing a strong second to Senator Clinton. There was plenty of indication that Edwards was on the rise.

Our surveys of Iowa showed consistent results prior to the release of the *Des Moines Register* poll. Each survey showed Edwards relatively strong as the voters' first choice in the survey and the overwhelming second choice for those caucus attendees whose first choice candidate was not receiving the required fifteen percent of the vote. As I noted, I really wasn't shocked when Brad Coker at Mason-Dixon, polling for MSNBC, showed Edwards in the lead. And there really seemed no way that Obama could overtake Clinton and Edwards, given the second-choice scenario. But that was before the phenomenally influential *Des Moines Register* poll was released.

Pollster J. Ann Selzer is unique in that Iowa polling is much of her business. Rather than jump to conspiratorial conclusions, let me set the arguments both in favor of and against Selzer's qualifications for conducting such a significant poll.

First, it appears by all accounts that Selzer is well qualified, smart, and probably understands Iowa politics better than anyone else in the research business. That all favors the idea that Selzer is perhaps the most qualified to conduct the poll for the largest newspaper in Iowa.

But is she too close to Iowa politics and politicians to defend attacks, real or imagined, based on who her clients are and in what direction their political philosophy leans? Possibly. Let me give some examples.

The Selzer & Co. web site listed the Des Moines-based State Public Policy Group as one of the dozen or so advocacy organizations for whom the company polls. Those who know the SPPG well say that the organization's COO, Jon Michael Rossman, was, going into 2008, known as the go-getter of the organization. He's a good example of the overall Democratic leaning makeup of the firm. He was also part of Barack Obama's original Generation Iowa steering committee.

Another of Selzer's clients, the Iowa Public Employees Retirement System, had the powerful Treasurer of the State of Iowa, Mike Fitzgerald, as a member of its board. He would be one of the state party's superdelegates to the Democratic National Convention. He also declared his support for Obama long before the Iowa caucus. Selzer's client list also included the Iowa State Education Association. Its president, Linda Nelson, endorsed Senator Obama in November 2007.

Selzer's client list was perfectly respectable, but it was primarily made up of a scattered number of newspapers around the nation and Iowa-based organizations, many fitting profiles similar to those listed above. These connections should not and do not impugn either Selzer's reputation or challenge her objectivity in polling the race. But, arguably, they could have made Selzer, who works with a relatively small circle of Democratic leaders in a relatively small state, sympathetic to the arguments being set forth for an Obama victory in Iowa. Those arguments included huge turnout by younger voters, massive participation by independent voters in the Democratic caucus, and a jump in overall turnout on January 3, 2008.

That certainly is the model that Selzer used in determining with her poll that Obama would basically cream the other candidates. The poll showed a staggering 32 percent to 25 percent lead for

Obama over Clinton, with Edwards at 24 percent. The result was like pouring gasoline on a fire. Suddenly Iowans were being told that they would turn out in record numbers, and that those who usually called themselves independent would join crossover Republicans to flood the caucuses and vote primarily for Obama.

If you want proof positive of the effect that the *Des Moines* poll had on the mindset of voters, you need look no further than the InsiderAdvantage poll we conducted in Iowa after the *Des Moines Register* poll had been released. Suddenly Obama gained among those who said he was their first choice. But much more important, of the voters whose first choice was clearly not going to make it after the fifteen percent cut, those who had a somewhat hazy but over-all opinion that Edwards was their second choice (sixty-two percent for Edwards, twenty-one percent for Clinton, seventeen percent for Obama as of December 29, 2007) completely flipped.

In a matter of a few days, voters were overwhelmingly for Obama. By our methodology, Obama suddenly had more than half of the voters who would be forced to make a second choice. The InsiderAdvantage poll, which was taken two days after the release of the *Register* poll, ended up being the last on the RealClearPolitics compilation. It showed Barack Obama ahead of the rest—by one point.

Was this because huge numbers of Hawkeye State voters had, in a matter of a few days, changed their opinion of Edwards? I doubt it. If anything, Edwards was being described by everyone on the campaign trail as being energetic and appealing to union members and rank-and-file, old-school Democrats in the more rural areas of the state.

It was clear to me that the *Des Moines Register* poll had the unintended effect of telling those who leaned towards Edwards that, in effect, their candidate had no prayer of winning and begged the question of why they would want to throw away their vote.

I'm not the only one who had significant questions about the methodology of the *Des Moines Register* poll or the impact it might have had on the outcome of the 2008 Iowa race. Dick Bennett of the New Hampshire-based polling firm American Research Group wrote in an online review after the Iowa Caucus that:

"Conventional wisdom on the Internet is that the final *Des Moines Register* poll accurately predicted the official outcome of the Democratic caucus. When the results of the *Des Moines Register* poll are compared to the result of the Democratic entrance poll, however, it becomes clear that the party composition of the *Register*'s Democratic sample was deeply flawed."

An examination of Selzer's *Des Moines Register* survey showed Selzer allocating around 40 percent of the likely Democratic caucus participants to individuals who were independent voters. She then allocated another seven percent or so to Republicans. That means that nearly half of those she included in the "weighting" of her dramatic poll were respondents who said they were not Democrats.

The exit polls proved that this methodology was way off base. According to exit poll results carried by MSNBC, only twenty percent of those who took part in the Iowa Democratic Caucus were independent voters. And only three percent were Republican. The poll had overstated participation by non-Democrats by a little more than double the ultimate percentage.

Barry Sussman, editor of the *Nieman Watchdog*, a publication of Harvard University's Nieman Foundation for Journalism, set forth numerous criticisms after the conclusion of the Iowa Caucus of the *Register* poll. He confirms what that editor in the mid-sized paper I described at the beginning of this chapter told me years earlier. Sussman notes that "bandied about over the years is the question of whether pre-election polls change voter behavior. If they do, it seems the change would be slight—but slight differences could result in different outcomes. For that reason alone, news organizations should be very cautious in their polling."

There is no doubt in my mind that the ultimate consequence of the *Register* poll, and I believe unintentionally so, was to change the dynamics of the race by giving Edwards voters, or those considering him as a second choice, no hope. Had Edwards split the second-choice vote with Clinton and Obama, Clinton would likely have come in first place in Iowa by a reasonable two to three points. Edwards would have remained a far more viable candidate, capable of fighting for significant votes in states such as South Carolina, which he had won just four years earlier.

Two truths about the 2008 *Des Moines Register* poll have become apparent. First, the poll undoubtedly set up a self-fulfilling prophecy. Second, there is no doubt that neither the paper nor the pollster in any way intended that to be the case.

But by using a methodology that put Obama substantially ahead of the rest of the candidates, the supporters of also-rans such as Sen. Christopher Dodd or Sen. Joe Biden likely felt no reason to fight Obama fever. They joined in and boarded the Obama upset train.

The American Research Group recalculated those results based on what they considered the flawed methodology of the *Des Moines Register* poll. They concluded that, using Selzer & Co.'s own "formula" as compared to the actual entrance poll percentages, the result of the last Iowa poll would or should have been Obama at thirty percent, Clinton at twenty-nine percent, and Edwards at twenty-four percent.

Of course, had the Selzer poll shown such a tight race, it is probable that the massive exodus of those critical "second-place" voters to Obama from the other candidates might well have never taken place. For Edwards, the poll was a political death sentence. And obviously, had confirmation of the rumors concerning Edward's relationship with a onetime campaign worker come to light, even wins in Iowa and beyond would have resulted in the same meltdown. But none of that had come to light in early January of 2008.

For Clinton, it was the first sign of the impact of the preconceived notions of the press and some pollsters as to what they expected to happen bumping up against—and likely changing—reality.

PART FIVE

PARANOID PRELIMS

★ 26 ★

"DON'T TOUCH ME"

When most of us who poll or chronicle political races started
looking at 2008 at least months in advance, we had no pre-
sumption that either major parties' nomination fights would be ter-
ribly close. And it was the Republicans who seemed more likely to go
down to a possibly brokered convention. That, if for no other reason
than that each GOP candidate had either a geographic or demographic area of strength. As for the Democrats, early front runner
Sen. Hillary Clinton looked likely to win the first few primaries and
never look back. We analysts had it something close to backwards.

In comparison to the extended Democratic war in 2008,
the Republicans fought only a few short battles. John McCain, of
course, was the man who in shockingly short order finished off his
opponents and nailed down the nomination for the GOP.

Florida's earlier-than-customary primary ensured that it
again would be a prime focus of attention in presidential politics, as
it had been especially in 2000. So CNN chose St. Petersburg, as the

place for a major Republican debate before the Christmas season temporarily diverted public attention from politics.

Following Arkansas Gov. Mike Huckabee's clear victory that night and the forthcoming avalanche of publicity it brought him, he started to overtake former Massachusetts Gov. Mitt Romney. Huckabee shot giant holes in Romney's social conservative base and left other candidates, namely Tennessee Sen. Fred Thompson, with only the picked-over remnants of the right-wing base to work with. He actually picked up some support from the more moderate independent-minded of Republican voters. Former New York City Mayor Rudy Giuliani was left floundering.

The key was Huckabee. He was keeping the under-funded McCain alive by splitting the conservative vote among himself, Romney, Thompson, and Giuliani. Self-identified social conservatives were telling us in our surveys that they were suddenly enamored with Huckabee. His good, old-fashioned combination of populism and pro-life sentiment offered these voters a more convincing brand of conservatism than the others.

So the Iowa caucus shaped up as a showdown between upstart Huckabee and the machine-politics operation of conservative designee Romney. Former fighter pilot John McCain was flying into the mix of things completely under the radar.

Some years previous, McCain had been speaking at a large conservative Christian organization's dinner. It was part of his concerted effort to repair the rift he had opened with conservative Christians during the bruising 2000 South Carolina primary against George W. Bush.

When it was time for McCain to take his seat at the head table, a grandmotherly figure—actually a shrewd, thick-skinned official of the Christian political movement—came upon the senator talking with a group of well-wishers. To get his attention and move him towards the dais, she clutched him by the shoulder.

"Don't touch me," he snapped. "Don't ever touch me." Flustered, the woman apologized and explained that they needed to move to the front of the room. McCain went right back to being his usual genial self but never apologized or explained his irritation.

This was in no way a shock. To anyone who had spent years being tortured as a prisoner of war, any sudden jab or grab might seem at least intrusive. Beyond that, it may simply have been a bad day for McCain. My own scattered personal encounters with McCain confirmed that he can run hot and cold. Even so, in my opinion, he was always composed.

One example: In the 2000 presidential campaign, McCain joined me and a colleague of mine on a half-hour TV broadcast from a local NBC affiliate. We covered many topics, including McCain's fervent desire to phase out production of the old war horse, Lockheed's C-130 Hercules military transport plane.

I had my own biases on the issue. My late uncle had been a test pilot for the Air Force and later for Lockheed. He'd flown the C-130 countless times and trained other pilots to do the same. Thanks to their ability to land on makeshift runways, the newer C-130s have continued to serve America well, including in Iraq and Afghanistan.

McCain and I had a heated exchange over his proposal to scrap the planes. "How can we spend money on these planes that are getting older and need parts when we have servicemen and women and their families on food stamps?" I recall McCain saying.

"But how many workers will you put on food stamps if you end production of the planes?" I shot back. We went round and round. McCain remained good-humored and gave as good as he got.

McCain knew that I was by then a "retired Republican." During the commercial break he looked at my co-host and joked, "I can't believe it. He's the Republican here!"

The lift that Mike Huckabee enjoyed after his solid performance in the November 2008 CNN/YouTube debate in St. Petersburg, coupled with the loads of press attention he got over the Christmas holidays, suddenly made him a front-runner in Iowa.

After Huckabee's win in Iowa, Mitt Romney and Rudy Giuliani were left reeling. Romney had forfeited much of the social conservative base to Huckabee. Giuliani, who would end up with a pitiful four percent of the vote in Iowa, was dead on arrival. And Fred Thompson, who ran a distant third in Iowa and came in second place but forty points behind Romney in the Nevada caucus, was picking up no steam whatsoever. Thompson was showing no signs of traction.

One could analyze the issues and positions and various debates to try to decipher how McCain, nearly broke and given up for politically dead going into Iowa, suddenly came to life and captured the one primary that is often considered essential to winning a party's nomination, New Hampshire.

It really came down to numbers and history: numbers in that Huckabee's sudden rise combined with Ron Paul's early strong showing to keep any of the more traditional conservative candidates from getting that critical, momentum-building early primary win, and history in that the precedent set by Ronald Reagan in 1980—of an outsider beating the GOP establishment—could happen again. The only compromise of that analogy is that in 2008, the "Reagan" would be a man, McCain, whose appeal to Republican conservatives was less than sterling.

Our firm chose not to poll in New Hampshire in 2008. We knew full well that New Hampshire is "The Contrarian State" politically. Voters there have a way of toying with pollsters. They did just that on the Democratic side in 2008. Most pollsters predicted an Obama victory. Clinton won.

For the Republicans, the pollsters did a commendable job. They not only got voters to talk on the phone, they got them to speak the truth. And the truth was obvious.

Although Southerner Huckabee looked to be too far to the right on social issues for the taste of New Hampshire—he would only win eleven percent of the vote—his performance was good enough to shear away critical votes from New England native son Romney. No one else would come close to McCain on primary night. As for moderates in this moderate Republican state, there was no one to speak of—and no one to split that vote with McCain.

Suddenly the pundits were starting to suggest that Huckabee might be a one-hit wonder. McCain was ordained the new hot candidate.

Romney would go on to win the small, GOP establishment-run Nevada caucus and the caucus in Michigan—where his father had once been governor, a state that most candidates would ignore in 2008. That left upcoming South Carolina as the true test for McCain's bid to become the alpha dog in the GOP pack.

★ 27 ★

SWEET REVENGE
AND SOUTHERN COMFORT

Team Romney fully expected that the media would put the spotlight on his Mormon faith just as their campaign would be rounding the third base of a home-run season in South Carolina. They assumed months earlier that their candidate would fare well in Iowa and win New Hampshire.

It's true that plenty of opposition research teams pored over The *Book of Mormon*, a sacred text of the Church of Jesus Christ of Latter Day Saints that is believed by Mormons to have been translated from ancient golden plates obtained from the Angel Moroni in rural New York in the early nineteenth century by Joseph Smith, Jr. The researchers were looking for passages that might prove troubling to Christian and secularist voters.

Inevitably, one of those passages would be from The *Book of Mormon*'s *Book of Nephi*. It portrays black skin as God's punishment for faithlessness. Until 1978, the church continued to refuse to ordain blacks into its lay priesthood, or to allow for blacks "proxy baptism," the church's practice of baptizing a living person on behalf of a dead person (including religious Jews). Such would be fodder for much media, especially if Romney were to win the Republican nomination.

Just a week or two before the South Carolina primary, I got a call from Ralph Reed (who I had known since we were kids), the man who had organized Christian conservative voters against John McCain in the 2000 South Carolina primary. Reed asked me to attend the premiere of *Amendment VI*, a documentary on which he'd been consulted. The film was about the role religion has played and will likely keep playing as a storyline in politics.

I brought along to the screening my longtime friend Gary Reese, who is also the editor of our *Florida Insider* publication. The film started at about 4:00 PM, and I was tired from so much polling and other work. I was afraid I might miss something, so I asked Gary ahead of time to be on the watch for subtle or even subliminal subject matter in the film.

Two good things happened to me that afternoon. First, I got a free bag of popcorn and a Coke just for showing up. Second, I caught a refreshing nap about twenty minutes into it.

Before I nodded off, Gary and I looked at each other and simultaneously whispered, "It's for Mitt." The documentary was a long disquisition on how one's religious beliefs should not be an impediment to holding the office of president.

But the picture, heavily promoted on national political web sites and slickly produced, never accomplished its goal. By the time Romney got to South Carolina, the combination of a stinging loss in Iowa to Huckabee and a humiliating setback to McCain in Romney's territory of New Hampshire made the news magazines' cover stories about Mormonism irrelevant.

While I'm sure the movie's producers had not coordinated their effort with the Romney campaign—or at least had kept enough distance to ensure legal protection—it was plain in my mind that some deep pockets supportive of Romney and paranoid about a potential "Mormon problem" had felt that the film had been worth plowing cash into.

The evolution of our company was such that, by 2008, we were more than a polling and research firm. We now owned several top electronic political news sites in the South, including the flagship *Southern Political Report*. This well-known newsletter had started as a print publication in 1978 under Hastings Wyman, a longtime DC insider.

By the time of the 2008 presidential campaign, we were also employing Tom Baxter, the former national editor and national political correspondent for the *Atlanta Journal-Constitution*, plus Lee Bandy, the legendary veteran political journalist for South Carolina's most influential newspaper, The *State*.

The South Carolina primary was slated for January 19, just eleven days after New Hampshire. Polling showed a tight race in the Palmetto State between McCain and Huckabee. McCain was taking the big military areas in a state where the military is critical, and Huckabee was surging in more socially conservative sectors of the state. That left Romney and Thompson with little, if anything, to fight over.

Our team fanned out across South Carolina. Tom Baxter appeared on MSNBC to discuss the close race. Lee Bandy was on FOX to describe the closeness of the race and to point out that unseasonably cold winter weather was expected on primary day.

Our polling surveys showed mixed results. Our electronic phoning system had yet to fail us, and it showed McCain and Huckabee tied within the poll's three-and-a-half-percent margin of error. Meanwhile, our live phone room poll proved once again why I have, over time, lost faith in traditional person-to-person polling interviews. It showed a ten-point lead for McCain. We threw these results in the trashcan.

Our electronic surveys are conducted with a professional taped voice. They are limited to less than three minutes and are written and programmed in a way that seems to make respondents feel very open about saying who they will vote for or if they are still undecided. This unique system has advanced to the point that we never doubt the results once they are properly weighted for age, race, gender, and other relevant factors.

On the day of the South Carolina primary, the state was hit with a cold rain mixed with some frozen precipitation. It didn't matter. Voter turnout was heavy.

McCain eked out a three-point win over Huckabee. Huckabee's close second finish was much as many pollsters had predicted, including us. But South Carolina proved a huge win for McCain in that he had conquered the very state that had destroyed his presidential campaign just eight years earlier. The crowd at his primary night victory party chanted, "Mac is back!" And he was.

McCain had captured South Carolina with the help of self-described independent voters. And Mike Huckabee, whose new political stardom was based on his performance at the CNN/YouTube debate in November, had once again deprived both the fading Romney and Thompson of much-needed conservative GOP votes.

Now the candidates headed back to Florida, where Huckabee's continued survival would prove problematic for a struggling Romney, who looked poised to be the most serious hanger-on challenger through the upcoming Super Tuesday slate of primaries.

But if Huckabee was problematic for most of the field, Florida's governor was potentially fatal for all but one candidate in that state's 2008 primary. Florida would prove to all but decide the race.

As the *St. Petersburg Times* political columnist had accurately reported months earlier, Florida's new political rock star, Gov. Charlie Crist, had been prepared to endorse Rudy Giuliani for president. But along about the time of the St. Petersburg GOP presidential debate in late 2007, Crist, who had been omnipresent just prior to the debate, was nowhere to be found, leaving Giuliani with no endorsement.

With an approval rating of over 75 percent, Charlie Crist had the power and influence that even former Florida Gov. Jeb Bush hadn't enjoyed when he helped nudge the Florida legislature to move the state's presidential primary to earlier in the calendar year.

After John McCain's victories in New Hampshire and South Carolina, Florida remained the last bastion of hope for Romney and the GOP Establishment.

Just days before the Florida primary, Crist found that his willingness to go along with the Bush-conceived early primary vote was a wise move. Now he was the kingmaker.

With just days to go before the Florida vote, Charlie Crist effectively decided the GOP nomination. He endorsed John McCain. An exit poll reported by CNN indicated that nearly forty percent of those who voted in the Florida Republican presidential primary said that the endorsement by their governor had an effect on their vote.

And so a plan hatched long before the actual primary, a plan whose architects likely had no idea that it would benefit upstart, independent-minded John McCain, resulted instead in the crowning Republicans' resident outsider as the unstoppable presumptive nominee of his party.

Just days later, I found myself sitting across from McCain on a smaller version of the now well-known "Straight Talk Express" bus. He had to be reveling in the knowledge that he was surely about to clean up during the GOP's version of Super Tuesday, thereby putting the final stake through the collective political hearts of his faltering Republican opponents.

On McCain's bus following a campaign rally were seated Sen. Lindsey Graham of South Carolina, Georgia Sen. Saxby Chambliss and his wife, and the wife of McCain's other close Senate buddy, Richard Burr of North Carolina.

For a few minutes I allowed myself to leave the world of non-partisan pundit and pollster and enjoy the feeling of the old days of my own Republicanism. It was like being back on an exhilarating campaign trail with a relaxed candidate after a heady event.

There really is nothing as enjoyable for those in my business than to be around political leaders when they know they are winning and can savor the moment. I put Sen. McCain on the phone with several of his former colleagues and associates. I joked a bit with Lindsey Graham and then watched as the McCains, Chamblisses, Graham, and Mrs. Burr posed for impromptu photos before one of those disposable cameras. All this was organized by Cindy McCain.

I couldn't help but think how happy McCain had to be. No matter what one's opinion of John McCain "the fighter" might have been, he as the gracious winner was enjoyable to watch. It was a fun ride on a winter's night in early February.

The road ahead would be less so for McCain. The heat of the summer and beyond was now waiting. He knew it and was readying himself.

★ 28 ★

A BRIEF HISTORY OF A REALLY LONG TIME:
OBAMA AND CLINTON FROM
NEW HAMPSHIRE TO WELL BEYOND

Following his wife's Iowa defeat, Bill Clinton moved to assert himself more in the strategy and direction of the campaign. The Rose Garden Coronation approach—giving the appearance that Hillary was essentially the incumbent president—had to be thrown out the window. The couple would now divide up and hit the road as "good" candidate (Hillary) and "bad" former president (Bill). Hillary would show signs of emotion, a behavior foreign to her public style. The former president would highlight what the Clinton team considered a pro-Obama biased media, thinking it would open the fight and put it back into the controlled hands of the Clinton machine.

After the demoralizing defeat in the Iowa caucus, and while fighting for her political life in New Hampshire, Hillary Clinton and her campaign decided that it was time to play to the strength that she had ignored to date: gender. In an episode that would come to exemplify a tough campaign and a tough cookie, Sen. Clinton reached the verge of tears in an interview with a female interviewer in Portsmouth, New Hampshire, on January 7. The tears may have welled up, however, but they never flowed. Hillary had to be Hillary.

At nearly the exact same time, in Hanover, Bill was lambasting the media for not pressing Senator Obama on his Iraq war voting record. In truth, the two candidates' records on the unpopular war were very similar.

Speaking in general about the press coverage of his wife and Obama, President Clinton said, "It's wrong that Senator Obama got to go through fifteen debates trumpeting his superior judgment [on Iraq]. . . . [Obama] said that in 2004 there was difference between Obama and George Bush on the war." Then, referring to an Obama campaign Web site that the president said substantiated the fact that the two candidates had differed on the war during their time in the Senate together, he added, "This whole thing is the biggest fairy tale I've ever seen."

Clinton's comments were the start of a string of statements that would leave him labeled a "loose cannon," even a bigot. He got accused of playing of the "race card" even though he never referenced Obama's race and his derogatory comments were directed entirely at the issue of the two candidates' war records. Clinton's statements would later be used against him. These characterizations would infuriate him. But in New Hampshire, where virtually every pollster had the contest in the Obama column, the combination of Hillary showing some human vulnerability and Bill Clinton taking off the gloves worked wonders. For the moment, the Clinton team had few regrets about their New Hampshire strategy.

Clinton raced up in the polls and defeated Obama in New Hampshire, even though not one major published poll showed her leading. It was an experience that confirmed my earlier intuition to not even try to take the pulse of New Hampshire voters. They are fiercely independent and often take pleasure in running contrary to the results in Iowa. They also get a kick out of confusing the pollsters during their moment in the political spotlight every four or eight years. (Good for them!)

Of course, the conspiracy types had their own answer for the New Hampshire result. A story carried on a popular news website, Presscue, claimed that the Clinton victory celebration was ". . . short-lived after Internet bloggers uncovered that the former first lady did better in precincts where votes were counted by the much-maligned Diebold voting machines, whereas in precincts where votes were hand-counted, her rival Barack Obama was the clear winner." The story went on that opinion polls had shown Obama had been way ahead, and that the actual, correctly counted vote reflected those polls! And this was written up as a new story.

I will confess that I was no fan of paperless voting when it was instituted. Many states have since decided to have some form of a paper record to accompany the electronic vote. But the Presscue story just shows how every aspect of politics can play to the paranoid side of the brain.

Because our polling firm had skipped New Hampshire, I could have sat back and chided other firms for missing the mark. But I don't think that would have been fair. The New Hampshire Democratic electorate went beyond simply asserting their contrarian independence. They also felt empathy, maybe even sympathy, for Hillary Clinton. Her supporters went to the polls in good numbers, and many undecided voters became decided in her favor.

Clinton would further her mini-comeback by carrying the Nevada caucus just days later. But what awaited her was the trap that now was becoming clear to the Clintons. The substantial number of delegates allocated to the Florida primary wouldn't matter. They weren't going to be counted in the delegate total. Momentum shifted and they would have to rely on South Carolina. Since the day Oprah Winfrey held her rally in the Palmetto State for Barack Obama, an African American electorate that had long loved the Clintons had found somebody new.

South Carolina's primary on January 19 was the next major primary after New Hampshire that would be counted in the delegate race, according to the Democratic National Committee's rules. (Michigan preceded South Carolina and Florida followed immediately after, but neither of those states delegates would be seated at the convention.)

The South Carolina contest loomed large as life for the Clintons. They knew they wouldn't have a prayer if South Carolina-born John Edwards was still actively in the race. Edwards had won South Carolina's primary just four years earlier. If he refused to leave the contest, the white vote would be significantly divided. Edwards didn't quit the race and, sure enough, white Democrats split their allegiance. Particularly in parts of the state that had lots of well-educated and well-heeled Democrats, the trend lines went for Obama. On the less affluent sides of town, whites divided between Clinton and Edwards. Obama got enough white votes, particularly in the big college town of Columbia, to combine with his overwhelming share of black votes, all to carry him to victory with fifty-five percent of the total.

It was in South Carolina where many in the media first chose to interpret Bill Clinton's attacks on Obama not as those of a realistic political expert fighting for his wife and her campaign, but instead as racist. To anyone who had dealt with Bill Clinton in past years, the concept was an absurdity. But to some Democrats, and to a certain group of journalists who were either suffering from a certain paranoia of their own or simply were too green to know better, Bill Clinton's South Carolina comments became proof that Clinton was injecting race into the primary contests.

On the day that Obama won the South Carolina primary, Bill Clinton was asked by reporters what it said about the Obama campaign that it took "both Clintons" to campaign against Obama in the state. Clinton said that Obama had run a good campaign and noted that Jesse Jackson had run a good campaign in 1984 and 1988 having once won the South Carolina primary himself.

Clinton's comparison of Obama to Jackson set off a firestorm of criticism. Yet Clinton was stating the obvious. One major network reported that Bill Clinton had "injected himself into the Democratic primary campaign with a series of inflammatory and negative statements." The report went on to suggest that while the alleged strategy might work, it might have in the long run damaged Clinton's reputation among African Americans.

In essence, Bill Clinton as the astute political observer had suddenly been turned into Bill Clinton the secret sympathizer with the KKK. The backlash seemed to have worked. The former president's magic would be declared to be "marginalized" by the pundits, at least until the end of the nomination process. But that really wasn't the case, as events in future contests would prove.

From South Carolina on January 19 through Super Tuesday on February 5—later renamed "Tsunami Tuesday" because a record twenty-four states and American Samoa held simultaneous caucuses or primaries—a pattern developed that never changed for the rest of the campaign season.

In states where the African American Democratic voting population was over thirty percent, Clinton faced major difficulties if not defeat. Obama was carrying between eighty to ninety percent of black voters in those states—Georgia, Alabama, Louisiana, and Virginia. All of them followed this basic pattern and fell Obama's way. He started out in each of those contests with anywhere between thirty to forty-five percent of the primary vote locked up before the first vote was cast. It killed the momentum for Clinton.

Meanwhile, smaller states with almost completely white electorates went for Obama as well. States such as Utah, North Dakota, Minnesota, Colorado, and Alaska all broke for Obama. Alone each state didn't mean very much, but with blowout percentages in many, Obama piled up delegates, and momentum.

Clinton's saving grace was in big states with white and Hispanic voter bases sizeable enough to outweigh any ninety-plus percent African American blocs for Obama, which by late February had become the norm.

The best examples of such break-out states were California and Texas. Clinton carried California on Super Tuesday, which some had polled earlier as an Obama win by a comfortable fifty-one percent to forty-one percent margin, with the remainder going to names no longer of significance. Her victory there would create the new argument that Hillary Clinton could carry the big states that Barack could not. Texas, with its mixture of Hispanic, African American, urban, and college-town white voters, plus rural but still Democratic-leaning whites, presented a pollster's nightmare. Our firm was the first of the major pollsters that consistently showed Clinton winning the Texas primary. Understandably, I was unsure of our numbers, which went against the popular grain. Many pundits also wondered about our numbers. And they had reason: liberal college towns such as Austin were likely to turn out in record numbers for Obama. My gut told me that Texas would be the beginning of the end for Clinton.

Clinton won by a fairly comfortable fifty-one percent to forty-seven percent margin. Again, huge support from Hispanics and women voters gave her the win.

But the better-organized Obama team, using its Facebook-style community organizations, stormed the state's caucus that was held after voting in the Texas primary ended, making Clinton's victory no real delegate boost.

After Obama's later win in Virginia on February 12, Clinton would have to wait until early May to have her first reasonable shot at not just a big win, but any win. Then came the famous "lunch bucket" vote of the Ohio primary.

Still behind substantially in delegates, Clinton needed a big win in this big state. With every pollster showing Clinton with a solid lead in Ohio, at our firm we again chose to sit the race out. No one needed a me-too poll, and we were still enjoying the feeling of having called Texas correctly in the face of a great deal of skepticism. In fact, only one pollster, Zogby, showed Obama tied with Clinton in

Ohio. It was not to be. Clinton blew Obama out of the water with a fifty-four percent to forty-five percent victory.

Despite Clinton's string of victories in big states, the damage of February and early March, plus the courage those events gave to super delegates to endorse Obama, all had Clinton fighting for her political life.

But just as it appeared Clinton was down for the count, the Obama campaign was hit with a version of the very sort of attack that Republican candidate Mitt Romney had so worried about but had never advanced far enough in the primaries to have to deal with: religion.

In Obama's case, it was not so much his religious faith per se as it was the words of his former pastor Jeremiah Wright that threatened his political career. An ABC News investigative story revealed past video sermons by Rev. Wright, Obama's longtime family minister at Chicago's Trinity United Church. One of the most controversial excerpts came from a sermon Wright delivered after the 9/11 attacks. Wright said that the United States's bombing of Hiroshima, Japan, in World War II was a far more reprehensible act than the World Trade Center and Pentagon bombings. Infamously, he said 9/11 was "America's chickens coming home to roost." Suddenly it wasn't Mormonism that was the "religious issue" of 2008.

Obama went through a baptism by fire after controversial comments of his pastor were made public. He kept his head down and survived, even after Wright made a second pass at gaining national media, reminding Americans of the tapes of him declaring, "Not God bless America, God damn America." Hey, if a candidate can withstand endless coverage of the man who ministered to his family for so many years with comments like Wright's, he must know how to deal with the press!

That's because media love only one thing more than a candidate they prefer—controversy. Still, in the critical days following the explosion of this controversy, Obama got some favorable reviews and polls that helped him steer clear of destruction.

When Obama on March 18 made a speech about his relationship with Wright, most press reviews gushed with praise for his artful handling of the situation. Many declared that Obama had put the issue to rest as quickly as it had arisen. Even though the speech was broadcast on television and was immediately available on Obama's web site and YouTube and, even though the full transcript appeared in both daily newspapers and on countless web sites, most people were not familiar with the speech.

Our firm polled the Wright issue at the same time as did other organizations and found that the controversy overall had a negative impact on opinions of Obama, providing they were aware of Wright's checkered career. Our poll didn't conclude that Wright necessarily changed minds about Obama. We just wanted to know if people were aware of the controversy, including Senator Obama's remarks about the former pastor and his own faith, and if they had, at that moment, had an effect on the campaign. The answer, not too surprisingly, was yes, and mostly negative.

I ran across the results of a CBS News poll conducted in the midst of the controversy. The article was one of the oddest things I had read in years—a perfect example of how the mixture of public opinion and news, if not carefully examined, can have confusing results.

In a release dated March 21, CBS released the results of a poll and characterized the results in the first lines of the release: "Most voters following the events regarding Senator Barack Obama and Rev. Jeremiah Wright think Obama's speech was a success."

The problem was that this wasn't what the poll said. It surveyed only those respondents who had either heard or read the actual words of Obama's speech in Philadelphia. Of those people—according to our own survey, a much smaller percentage than those aware of the whole controversy—sixty-nine percent said the speech was a success. But that was a much smaller slice of the overall American opinion pie than put forth by CBS in the first lines of its release.

What made the CBS survey unreliable was that they surveyed a set group of respondents about their opinions before the speech, then called the same respondents to seek their opinion about the speech. In other words, this was not some random sample, but instead a highly focused group that was polled and re-polled.

Do I believe the people at CBS got together in some grand conspiracy and decided to manufacture the news as they wanted it? No. But I thought it irresponsible not to notice the obvious disconnect between going back to people that one knows are going to watch or listen to a speech, and then declaring that sixty-nine percent that had heard or read about the speech had a favorable impression. What was worse was then extrapolating the poll even further to suggest that the speech was a hit with sixty-nine percent of all voters.

Conspiracy? Absolutely not. As Jody Powell put it in a book I co-authored several years ago entitled *Mean Business: The Insider's Guide to Winning Any Political Election*, "There is a desperate human need to impose order on any chaotic situation, when there may be no order there, even in political campaigns. . . . My longtime observation is that any time you have a chance of betting on a conspiracy theory of history or the screw-up theory of history, bet on the screw-up. You will probably be right."

In the case of the CBS News poll, my bet is on the screw-up. My guess is that, just like in every organization big or small, CBS simply screwed up by failing to note that a group of highly aware pre-polled respondents, when polled again, would be more likely to pay attention to Obama's speech. Even if their opinion was correct, it could not be stated that it represented the opinion of voters overall. But the impact certainly helped Sen. Obama, as did similar surveys that focused the respondents' attention on a specific speech rather than on the controversy as a whole. It helped Obama, but not enough to keep him from having to work even harder to stave off a newly recharged Clinton machine.

On Friday morning of April 18, in the *Wall Street Journal* I read the headline, "Clinton's Goal: Win Big in Pennsylvania, Sow Doubts Over Obama." Bleary-eyed, I scanned the story for what I assumed would be the obvious. Reporter Amy Chozick indicated that Clinton's lead in Pennsylvania, over ten points just a month previous—and still over ten points in the most recent SurveyUSA poll, and between seven percent and ten percent in our InsiderAdvantage survey—had dwindled to single digits in other surveys, suggesting a big win for Clinton was looking less likely.

Chozick summarized Clinton's problem: "A large victory would help the Clinton campaign drum up donations and offset what may be a weak showing in the North Carolina contest where an Insider Advantage [sic] poll of likely voters released earlier this week put Senator Obama ahead by a fifteen percent margin."

My eyes brightened. Once again our polling numbers were being correctly interpreted to show there was little hope left for the Clinton team. And they knew it. An April 22 Clinton win in delegate-rich Pennsylvania would have to be overwhelming. And on this same Black Friday for the Clinton campaign, more key Democratic leaders announced their endorsement of Obama. They ranged from diminutive Clinton protégé Robert Reich to the oft-described moderate former Southern Democratic Senator Sam Nunn of Georgia, who announced that he felt more comfortable with Obama's view of the international landscape and respected the candidate's devotion to change. Even those on the fringe of the Democratic elite were attempting to place a marker, betting that Pennsylvania would indeed be close and would ultimately be the end of the road for Clinton.

Earlier that week ABC News had broadcast a highly viewed debate between Clinton and Obama. The results were predictable. Almost before the discussion had ended, Obama supporters such as Tom Shales, television critic for the *Washington Post*, assailed the moderators for being too hard on their candidate. They called it shameless.

They especially blamed former Clinton White House official George Stephanopoulos and ABC anchor Charlie Gibson for focusing too much on a few controversial statements made by Obama, especially some then-hot comments from a San Francisco fundraiser. Fresh from a tour of Pennsylvania, Obama had described small-town Americans as "bitter" and, in response to tough economic times, as "clinging to guns and religion." Those criticizing the ABC News debate did so ignoring the fact that when Clinton had been brutalized in debates earlier in the season, the one-sidedness was so apparent that television's *Saturday Night Live* felt compelled to lampoon the events, with mock moderators drilling Amy Poehler's Clinton character with scathing questions, while asking Fred Armisen's Obama character if he was comfy, or needed a glass of water, or a pillow.

Obviously the elite media couldn't take it that Barack Obama was being manhandled in the same way Clinton had been. Rather than admit that his performance in the debate was at best mediocre, they chose to attack ABC News. It didn't work.

I watched the debate and thought it more civil and policy-driven than most of the debates I had viewed throughout the 2007-2008 campaigns. It also received the highest ratings of any of the debates of the long presidential primary season. I communicated briefly with Stephanopoulos telling him to hang in there. I noted that given my past close association with Newt Gingrich and other Republicans, I could never convince the networks or newspapers that I didn't have a secret agenda. (And I didn't, other than perhaps to throttle Newt's neck from time to time.) George, always a gentleman, responded immediately with his appreciation. He is lucky though. He worked for a Democratic president. No matter how hard he might work to play things down the middle—and I believe he is diligent about doing so—had he been a part of a Republican administration, there is no doubt in my mind that he would not be hosting a Sunday political talk show for one of the major broadcast networks. Even George couldn't pass the Chinese water torture administered to former Republicans when it comes to being viewed as responsible "mainstream" media.

As the Pennsylvania primary approached, much of the press made another huge miscalculation. While they generally were acknowledging that Clinton would win the primary, they emphasized, once again, that the vote from the southern part of the state, Philadelphia in particular, would be heavily pro-Obama. The new spin was that Hillary Clinton had to have a huge margin of victory in Pennsylvania or she was finished.

Clinton and Obama battled furiously in the last weekend before the vote. Obama chose to remain fiercely engaged in the fight there despite knowing that he would lose. His campaign's own internal numbers fluctuated wildly, but near the end of the weekend he had reason to believe he would narrow Clinton's lead and potentially keep her to a four-point victory or less. That would be the magic bullet which would allow the unbound super delegates to say in unison that the race had to come to an end and Clinton had to get out.

Clinton stressed her family ties to Scranton and tried to cultivate an image of herself as a woman of the people. She downed whiskey and beer and donned her trademark pantsuits to wade into the masses of Pennsylvania more like a hard-bitten Rocky Balboa than a Wellesley- and Yale-educated policy wonk. MSNBC's Chris Matthews quipped that "most people now think that Hillary Clinton got a G.E.D. from somewhere in Scranton." Matthews has been in the world of big-time, behind-the-scenes politics for a long time, and he could spot a slick move in a heartbeat.

As the final days before the Pennsylvania primary drew to a close, Hillary Clinton was part underdog scrapper, part Energizer Bunny. Barack Obama was a reluctant fighter whose energy had waned.

Cynthia Tucker, the Pulitzer Prize-winning editorial page editor of the *Atlanta Journal-Constitution*, nailed Obama's real problem: He had failed to use humor to diffuse the Clintons. After all, Clinton, the spurned woman, could afford to seem tough, but Obama, the black male, could never afford to risk being the "Angry Black Man."

And that's where another of Bill Clinton's much-discussed, loose-cannon episodes came into play. In a radio interview the Monday before the election, he clearly said that the Obama campaign had "played the race card" on him after the South Carolina primary. He said that his comments comparing Obama's South Carolina primary victory to that of Jesse Jackson's years earlier had been twisted by the press. Said Obama, "Hold on a second. So former President Clinton dismissed my victory in South Carolina as being similar to Jesse Jackson, and he's suggesting that somehow I had something to do with it? . . . OK, well, you better ask him what he meant by that."

But Clinton declared, "No, I think that they played the race card on me. . . . We now know from memos from the campaign and everything that they planned to do it all along."

The next morning, when asked about the comments, Clinton indignantly confronted a television reporter saying, "You always follow me around and play these little games and I'm not going to play your game today. This is a day about Election Day."

In private, Bill Clinton was comfortable with his efforts. He was trying to push Obama over the edge, to make him grim and nasty. And he was getting even for what clearly had been unfair portrayals of his comments during the nomination process. Clinton was attempting to sandbag the seemingly green and inexperienced one-term senator into the same tailspin of negativity and anger that had haunted Senator Clinton until her Texas turnaround. Most of all, Clinton got Obama talking about a name anathema among white Pennsylvania voters on the very day that they were headed to the polls—Jesse Jackson.

The bait had been taken. Bill Clinton's plan was working brilliantly, just as it had in New Hampshire. Obama was on the defensive and off his positive message; he was talking about Jesse Jackson. As one observer put it, "I'm so confused I don't know who is playing the race card more or at the wrong time. Bill Clinton seems on it in South Carolina where the black voters rule, and now Barack is talking about it in a state where he needs white votes . . . it's crazy." But it was Bill Clinton who caught the wrath of the media.

The pundits and media pounced. To almost everyone, President Clinton seemed to be making one amateurish misstep after another. Why, the experts on the Sunday political talk shows asked, would he squander the legacy of his presidency and his relationship with the black community in such a reckless fashion? Even a week later, top writers and experts were wondering if Bill Clinton had become such a distraction to the campaign that he needed to be muzzled or repudiated.

They didn't get it. How could they have forgotten that his was the sharpest strategic and tactical mind in contemporary American politics? The former president had already discerned that the Clintons' earlier softer approach had been a huge mistake after the Iowa results rolled in. Now Bill would have to become the sacrificial lamb. He determined that he would have to undertake the role filled by James Carville in his own campaigns; that of the human lightening rod.

Bill Clinton could rebuild his legacy regardless of whether his wife won or not. After all, Obama would need the public support of Bill and Hillary. But still hoping for Hillary to win, Bill would see Obama crawling on his knees begging for support from women age fifty and over. The president knew that the more he focused on Obama's image in the media—from euphoric "agent of change" to defensive frontrunner who couldn't connect with "real Democrats"—the greater the chance that Hillary could pull off a Hail Mary. Barring his wife's nomination, former President Clinton wanted to see that Hillary retained maximum clout when Obama began considering running mates, cabinet members, ambassadors and the like.

For Barack Obama it was all about winning the presidency. For those backing him it was about power. For the Clintons it was always about power, no matter what the title. It was the real game, the only one that matters in the business, and Bill Clinton had come to realize that no one had clued Obama in on this secret.

The Pennsylvania primary would leave lingering doubts that would remain all the way to the very last days of the general election in November. It would raise questions such as whether poll results showing strong performances by Obama in states like Pennsylvania would actually hold up on election day. It would also call into question a more haunting issue for the Democratic Party: was the party more plagued by issues related to race and gender than was the nation as a whole?

On primary election night, as the first exit polls suggested just what Obama needed—a fifty-two percent to forty-eight percent lead over Clinton—the major cable and broadcast networks began running the crawls that the Obama team so very much wanted to see: "Race too close to call in Pennsylvania." Analysts on CNN were already talking about the potential impact such an underperformance in Pennsylvania might have on Clinton. As they broke down the exit poll demographics, things looked grim for Clinton. Over ninety percent of African Americans had voted for Obama. Men had gone for him as well. Clinton, based on the exit polls, could only claim women and seniors as her base. Everything that was being reported would certainly support a slim win by Clinton. There was only one thing. The exit polls were, as usual, wrong.

As results from the bedroom communities outside Philadelphia—the so-called "Springsteen Generation" that supposedly would hugely support Obama—began to come in, it was clear that Obama would suffer a big defeat. He carried few counties in the state. The working man and woman had shunned his candidacy in a big way. While the exit polls seemed to suggest many voters waited until the last minute to decide, and that those voters went strongly for Obama, the prior polling and sheer logic told one that this simply was not the case.

In the last round of polling before the Pennsylvania showdown, every major pollster had Clinton wining. Our last two InsiderAdvantage polls, taken on Sunday and Monday nights before the Tuesday election, showed Clinton with a ten percent and a seven percent lead respectively. Zogby showed a last-minute ten-point lead for Clinton as well. We all had remaining undecided voters in our surveys. But wait a minute: Clinton won with 54.6 percent of the vote compared to Obama's 45.4 percent. How could the undecided voters have broken for Obama?

They didn't. In our last poll in the race, InsiderAdvantage showed forty-nine percent for Clinton and forty-two percent for Obama, with between eight or nine percent undecided. Zogby had the race at fifty-one percent for Clinton to forty-one percent for Obama, with eight percent undecided. Quinnipiac University had the race at fifty-one percent for Clinton to forty-four percent for Obama. Suffolk had the race at fifty-two percent to forty-two percent, again with Clinton in the lead. Other pollsters either had the race much closer or had not polled in the final two days. So do the math.

According to our InsiderAdvantage poll, Clinton would have to have picked up the lion's share of the undecided voters to get to 54.6 percent. Using Zogby's numbers it would basically have been an even split of the undecided voters. In the Quinnipiac poll, to reach the final result, Obama would have gained none of the undecideds. It was the same for the Suffolk poll.

The undecided vote moved slowly downward between our Sunday night survey and our Monday night round of polling. Since both samples had virtually the same number of respondents, it was fair to conclude that the last-minute voters were moving more in Obama's direction. That said, from my experience, if a voter is still undecided the day before a race, they likely are not voting.

Before the contest, I projected Pennsylvania as a fifty-three percent or fifty-four percent Clinton win. The only way it could have been much closer was if this race had been so intense that the undecideds in the poll truly were undecided and they continued to break for Obama. Were that the case, Clinton would have won by a much smaller margin, perhaps as little as two or three percent. Obama's team was betting on this scenario, while Clinton's folks were hoping that, as far as the undecideds that remained, they would behave as usual and not vote.

But one would never have known this after reading the Sunday papers the weekend after the Pennsylvania Clinton romp. In looking towards the Indiana primary, columnists pointed again and again to the flawed Pennsylvania exit polls that somehow created the misimpression that Hillary and Bill Clinton had turned voters off just a little too late for an Obama win, but that the big turn of undecided voters in Pennsylvania towards Obama was a trend to look for in Indiana. A trend that, combined with a tough North Carolina race, would create the beginning of the end for Hillary Clinton's quest for the nomination.

★ 29 ★

CLOSE, BUT NO . . .

The trend to look for in Indiana was a return performance of J. Ann Selzer of *Des Moines Register* polling fame. But this time her unique "model" of a turnout of inspired young people and educated liberals flooding into the streets would not work. Indiana, despite the fact that it, like its neighboring Iowa, is dominated by a small number of newspapers and could be viewed to be a more diverse version of Iowa, would not fall prey to another Selzer moment like that of the *Des Moines Register* poll.

But it wasn't like it didn't start out that way.

With Clinton's huge Pennsylvania victory, pundits, including me, wrote that Obama would have an easy time in North Carolina. That state has a high African American population and a white Democratic profile dominated by that state's Research Triangle intellectuals.

Our initial polling of the North Carolina primary—to be held along with Indiana on May 6—showed Clinton getting clobbered by fourteen points. The media thought that Obama would take Indiana as well and finally send a message to the Clintons to fold their tent and end the nightmare. Selzer's poll for the *Indianapolis Star* showed Obama leading in late April, despite the Clinton momentum from the Pennsylvania win. The pundits made it clear: A double defeat and it was the end for Clinton.

But there were several things already at work that Selzer and others were not picking up on. First, the disconnect between working-class whites and Obama was growing even as the Pennsylvania vote was still fresh in the public's mind. And second, the newly reinvigorated Clintons were showing a willingness to gut-fight, using every last trick and ounce of energy they had.

What happened next became one of the biggest political stories of the Democratic fight for the nomination. It too would become fodder for those tempted to find conspiracies lurking in the dark shadow of politics. This time the conspiracy theories would come from the very establishment elite who pooh-poohed such rubbish in virtually every instance.

In a series of media bursts, beginning with a tepid interview with Charlie Rose on PBS and ending in one of the most bizarre performances ever seen at the Washington Press Club, the Rev. Jeremiah Wright arose like Lazarus and came forth. And he was certainly in his full glory.

Obama's former pastor, answering questions put to him by a moderator, as is the press club's custom, paced back and forth behind her almost like a bull in the chute. With each question his pacing became more rapid and pronounced. Each answer received laughs and applause.

Within a matter of hours the more sophisticated in the Obama circle felt they might well have been had by a sly contingent of Clinton supporters who somehow got to Wright during the period he had been forced to go on the down-low to avoid media questions about his many controversial sermons and statements. After all, what happened to change the reverend's demeanor from that of recluse unavailable for comment to a media motor mouth?

"If you don't think we think they got to him, you have another thing coming," said a well-connected Obama supporter. They felt it was clear. The allegation was that the old "here's-a-contract" routine had been put to the reverend. You help attorney so-and-so as he consults for a mega "outreach" group as a consultant on some initiative far from Chicago. You sign a non-disclosure agreement, and, by the way, wouldn't it be good if you told your side of the story?

Few in the Obama camp believed Rev. Wright felt so disrespected that he would not have stayed the course, let things blow over, rehabilitate himself quietly in the coming months, and enjoy the almost inevitable rapprochement with Obama and his family, once in the White House. But as usual, their guessing could be true or just coincidental odd behavior by Wright.

Obama insiders noticed that the Clintons had scheduled an appearance on FOX News's The *O'Reilly Factor* on the very night of the Washington Press Club speech. "Give me a break," my source in the Obama campaign shouted, "Bill O'Reilly's always called Hillary a socialist. Now they suddenly manage to schedule this thing for the exact same week, the exact same day?"

Convinced they had been betrayed by Wright, and not just because the reverend felt wronged, but because, in their mind, he might have been a bought-and-paid-for Judas, the Obama camp cut all ties with their former pastor. "You see," said one veteran of the civil rights movement, "it seems that every great black leader has their Judas. Martin [Luther King, Jr.] did and, in our opinion it's looking like Jeremiah Wright has taken the ultimate in street money . . . all bundled up by some really slick lawyers."

Rumors ran rampant, chief among them that longtime Clinton confidante, attorney, and political powerbroker Vernon Jordan had somehow helped arrange Wright's Press Club appearance. Regardless of the validity of the rumors and conspiracy theories, the damage from Wright spread not only to Indiana, but hit directly at the state where Obama was expected to gain a double-digit win just a week later, North Carolina.

Our polls in North Carolina, like most other polls of the race, had shown Obama winning by double digits prior to the Wright comments. Our earlier polls had projected Obama winning the white vote in the Tar Heel State by a comfortable margin. Wednesday morning, just six days from the vote, I received the weighted summary of our poll conducted the night before. This was a poll that surveyed North Carolina one full day after the circus performance by Wright at the Washington Press Club. I was stunned.

White Democratic voters in North Carolina had shifted overwhelmingly to Clinton. And because InsideAdvantage's surveys are particularly strong in our native South, where we poll often and know that black respondents regularly refrain from giving their final voting choice, we projected blacks supporting Obama far below the usual eighty percent to ninety percent. Consequently, we showed Hillary Clinton, within the margin of error, leading Obama in North Carolina.

That night, appearing on FOX News' *Hannity and Colmes* with pollster Scott Rasmussen, I explained that the numbers of African American voters going for Obama would probably increase and that he would likely win the North Carolina contest. But, I argued, it wouldn't be by the fourteen percent margin Rasmussen's poll of the night before had shown. He agreed. We both felt that the final number would meet somewhere in the middle. Indeed, just two days later our poll had Obama up by five percent.

On the Saturday before the North Carolina vote, David Gergen, appearing on CNN, said that any win by Obama in North Carolina would be significant and would basically force the hand of the Clinton campaign to yield to the will of party leaders and quit. Gone were the proclamations that Indiana was the one and only determining state left on the table. That was because, other than in a Zogby poll, Indiana appeared to be moving increasingly towards Clinton.

But what everyone was missing in looking at these races was the big picture. Even a tighter North Carolina race could never give Hillary Clinton the delegates she needed to catch up to her opponent. And a victory in Indiana wouldn't do the trick either. The final vote results on May 6 showed a fourteen-point victory for Obama in North Carolina and two-point victory for Clinton in Indiana.

Not enough. Not enough to stop an increasing number of party leaders from pleading for an end to the battles. Not enough even with the huge Clinton victories that followed in Kentucky and delegate-rich Puerto Rico.

In the greatest irony of the campaign, Hillary Clinton, virtually anointed a year earlier, watched as results from Montana, one of the least populated states in the nation, combined with a further move of super delegates to Obama, making Obama the presumed nominee. The most open presidential primary season in modern history was finally won. But yet there were still more questions than answers in the minds of the politicians, the press and an unusually engaged public.

PART SIX

UNCONVENTIONAL MOVES

★ 30 ★

STRANGE BEDFELLOWS

The Republican establishment was on its heels with the presumptive nomination of John McCain as the party's nominee. As springtime moved towards summer, the campaign was still in the hands of longtime McCain loyalist Rick Davis.

As with most GOP operatives, one could find Davis's ties to the national GOP and Bush during the years George W. Bush held office. Even so, Davis was viewed by Republican insiders as very much an outsider when it came to the real party elite. He came from "the Dole side" of the party, having assisted longtime GOP stalwart and lobbyist Paul Manafort in managing the 1996 Republican National Convention in San Diego. That year, the Manafort team gave it their all in a valiant try at putting some zest into a Bob Dole campaign that was a victim of not being a part of the old-line GOP establishment group.

Like McCain, Dole was independent, could shoot from the hip, and had a cracking sense of humor. All three happened to be characteristics not in keeping with blueblood Republicanism.

In working for Manafort, Davis had done everything possible to help Dole. But one could feel the lack of excitement from a critical wing of the Republican Party—those with most of the money—even in the naturally optimistic setting of sunny San Diego that year. In an effort to energize the Dole campaign, former New York Congressman and U.S. Secretary of Housing and Urban Development Jack Kemp was named Dole's vice presidential nominee.

There were few of us who knew Jack Kemp who didn't also like him. Jack had campaigned for me in 1990 when I was the Republican nominee for lieutenant governor of Georgia. He was a true grassroots conservative with boundless energy and a gift for gab virtually unequalled.

Years earlier, my wife and I were giving Jack a ride to an airport. Knowing that Kemp and Newt Gingrich were good friends, I couldn't help but laugh when Jack said something to the effect of, "Newt has great ideas, but sometimes I just wish we could get him not to talk so much and quit saying everything that's on his mind." We waited until we let him out of the car to laugh. Anyone who knew Jack Kemp knew that he and Gingrich were two peas in a pod when it came to being loquacious. This was truly the pot calling the kettle black.

I don't recall ever meeting or knowing Rick Davis, but our mutual acquaintances say nothing but good things about him. I know that as he worked behind the scenes of the 1996 convention, where Newt was the presiding officer, I could feel good vibrations from the effort—but little real hope. I stood watching as Dole and Kemp were dramatically brought into San Diego on some sort of boat. And I remember telling one of our (Newt's) people how happy I was to see two really good guys coming in to be named the leaders of the GOP. "But," I remember noting, "that boat might as well say *S.S. Titanic*, because there is no way we are ever going to get the money guys to be with us."

Dole and Kemp were swamped by the Clinton-Gore reelection machine just months later. And for the most part, the GOP establishment sat on its hands and watched the defeat unfold from the sidelines.

By 1999, Rick Davis had signed on with John McCain's 2000 effort to win the Republican nomination. That would make two strikes in favor of Davis as an independent and loyal guy, and two against him for bucking the party establishment. The 2000 GOP fight for the nomination would become a bitter one between George W. Bush and John McCain.

In 2000, McCain focused most of his primary campaign strategy on winning New Hampshire. Creating his first "Straight Talk Express" with Davis and other "maverick" political operatives such as longtime McCain confidante John Weaver, the team demanded to be taken seriously by the Bush establishment when McCain upset George W. in the New Hampshire primary.

Suddenly the establishment's "hard work of not working hard" on behalf of Dole in 1996, combined with the now genuine effort to raise money and create a winning organization for George W. Bush, was all threatening to get derailed by the upstart McCain. (George W. Bush was then governor of Texas, but "Junior" or "W" was looked upon by the GOP inner circle as a sort of cowboy version of daddy George H. W. Bush.)

The battleground to stave off McCain in 2000 would be the South Carolina primary. And Bush had assembled a tight-knit group of political pros who knew South Carolina like natives.

Their lead dog in South Carolina would be a political consultant I had hired years earlier in a governor's race, Warren Tompkins. He was known for his brilliantly aggressive brand of politics. Unfortunately I never really got to see it in action. Just as our race seemed to be tanking in its closing weeks, our campaign sent a car to pick up Tompkins, who was supposed to arrive at the airport for a last-ditch strategy session. At last check, the driver we dispatched to pick him up was still standing by the car waiting for the no-show Tompkins. (The race ended in a near-upset, not the embarrassing stomping Tompkins thought he faced.)

There were other big names involved in the South Carolina effort. Ralph Reed was highly active. He organized evangelical voters in the state for Bush.

But South Carolina still posed a problem for the Bush team, not least because of its many military and ex-military voters who might be inclined to vote for the military hero McCain.

The ultimate difference may have been a massive "push poll" that asked voters, "Would you be more likely to vote for John McCain if you knew he had fathered an illegitimate black child?" Allegedly, the poll targeted hundreds of thousands of households right before the Republican primary vote and was credited as a move that brought South Carolina home for Bush in 2000.

Many top McCain strategists said both on and off the record that it was Bush campaign manager and later top White House advisor Karl Rove who masterminded the so-called push poll. Whether true or not, the belief was there.

Now fast-forward to 2008, and the question was unavoidable: Is there any way the candidates and consultants from that 2000 race could trust each other in 2008?

The quick answer had to be no. But politics makes strange bedfellows, and cash-poor candidates can sometimes be forced to forge alliances with all sorts of political characters, trustworthy or not.

In the 2007 early goings of the presidential race, John McCain was truly that needy candidate. In July 2007 he was almost completely out of money. His most loyal advisors, like John Weaver, left the campaign. Rick Davis would become the campaign manager, but it would take the set of miracles that later unfolded to bring McCain back to a position of strength as the party's likely nominee.

McCain discovered that even being the Republicans' presumptive nominee didn't necessarily bring the party establishment's purse strings along with it. Recall that McCain had already pledged to take Federal funding for his campaign. Now he had precious little time to entice the big-dollar Bush crowd before the bell would sound and he could no longer accept deep-pocket contributions under the rules of the Federal financing of presidential campaigns.

These finance rules would not hinder Obama. In light of his unprecedented fundraising prowess, he decided that it was no longer attractive to stick to his earlier pledge to adopt the same public financing of his general election effort that McCain had.

McCain had secured wealthy Cincinnati investor/businessman Mercer Reynolds as his new marquee leader. Reynolds had chaired a record fundraising effort for his close friend George W. Bush in 2004. Reynolds would be McCain's finance chair now that the Republican nomination was locked up. It was clear that McCain would have to do more than rock the GOP boat a little if he wanted to compete with Obama's aircraft carrier of financial might.

In 2004 Reynolds and his team created a cadre of "bundlers." Those were people who could raise large amounts of cash as a series of individual donations. That allowed them prestigious designations such as Rangers or Pioneers within the Bush organization.

But by early July 2008 the *Arizona Republic* reported a curious set of figures. The newspaper noted that, as of the then-latest campaign finance reports:

"McCain has at least 507 bundlers. . . . That is nearly as many as the 557 identified bundlers Bush had during the 2004 campaign. But Bush had far greater success raising money than McCain is having. . .Four years ago, Bush had raised $209 million by the end of May. McCain reported raising $111 million through May."

The squeeze was on. The money spigot simply would not open up until McCain made it clear that his "maverick" persona would have a lot more of a Bush-like flavor before the campaign was over.

The end game for the GOP's old guard was to see Mitt Romney placed on the ticket with McCain. To gain that money, it seemed likely that McCain would have to give strong hints that he would not only dance with those who had once fought him, but that he would marry up with one of their own as his running mate.

In the interim, it seemed critical for the Bush organization to seize greater control of the McCain operation. A series of missteps by McCain's staff fueled this strategy. Among those gaffes were allowing McCain to make off-the-cuff remarks that made him seem amateurish on the economy and standing by as he made slow responses to various issues raised by Obama.

All this opened the door for longtime Bush/Rove loyalist Steve Schmidt to move to the role of day-to-day operations director for the McCain campaign. Rick Davis was still a critical part of the McCain team. But everyone now knew who would ultimately be calling the shots on a minute-by-minute basis. Schmidt.

Not that he lacked loyalty to his candidate. He joined the McCain effort when it was still in its exploratory stage, and his addition was praised by none other than John Weaver at the time. Schmidt returned the favor the following year when Weaver, who had left the McCain campaign, was accused of leaking a story to the *New York Times*. It came out during the heated primary season and said that McCain had allegedly had a romantic relationship with a young woman lobbyist in prior years. The story was a flash in the pan that never developed but left the clear impression on observers that the man who was at one time best known as John McCain's closest advisor and a maverick himself—Weaver—was no longer in McCain's inner circle. And he was being defended by a longtime Bushie.

That was more significant than most realized. Weaver had been willing to join causes and work on efforts for McCain that would have jeopardized the Republican careers of most during the Bush years. I know because for several years both Weaver and I worked with a client whose cause seemed just, but who was despised by the Bush White House. I recall only one or two conference call discussions with Weaver, but it was enough to size him up as a guy who wasn't afraid to take on the GOP establishment. And he was completely devoted to McCain.

Steve Schmidt's bloodline ran directly to Rove and Bush. He had served as Deputy Assistant to the President and Counselor to the Vice President in George W. Bush's White House. He went on to run the "war room" for the 2004 reelection campaign.

One of Schmidt's first hires was fellow Rove/Bush devotee Mike McDonald. So in short order, the maverick campaign of John McCain had all the trappings of a third election run by George W. Bush.

On July 2, 2008, the day that Schmidt's promotion was announced, a Gallup poll showed John McCain trailing Barack Obama by four points nationally. In mid-October, Colin Powell endorsed Barack Obama. Powell had been National Security Adviser to George H.W. Bush and Chairman of the Joint Chiefs of Staff and later Secretary of State to George W. Bush. When this declaration of support came, McCain still trailed Obama in the Gallup poll— by the same four percent as more than three months previous.

Also in mid-October Bill Kristol, Editor of the *Weekly Standard* and one of the savviest minds in Washington, told the television program *Fox & Friends* that the entire McCain staff should be fired:

"McCain should forget about all the staff management. Every place he goes he should do a press conference. He should do all the local TV, he should do talk radio. They should let them be themselves. . . they've managed to bottle them up, make them look negative. . . I think it's foolish and it's not working."

By "them," Kristol was referring to McCain plus a woman few had heard of prior to the Republican National Convention in early September—Sarah Palin. And Kristol was right. Since the Republican presidential ticket had been announced in St. Paul, the

GOP nominee and his running mate had appeared, according to the *Wall Street Journal*—as of the same day that Kristol made his statement— in forty fewer campaign events than their Democratic counterparts had in states where the race was contested.

Was there a reason for this strategy? Perhaps the story of Alaska Governor Palin could help shed light on the situation.

But to get to the name Sarah Palin, one would first have to pass through two other far-better-known names, each of whom thought he was destined to be McCain's running-mate.

★ 31 ★

PARANOID "PASSOVER"

It was hard in 2008 to imagine that Connecticut Democratic Senator Joe Lieberman was former Vice President Al Gore's running-mate just eight years earlier. Remember that it was Lieberman and Gore who—according to many—had been the victims of the greatest political conspiracy in American history, the "stealing" of a presidential election in Florida, where the Republican nominee's brother had been the governor.

The story of that frantic turmoil started out with hanging and dimpled chads and then wound its way through decisions by county election boards, lower state courts, the Florida Supreme Court, and finally the U.S. Supreme Court. The tale of intrigue and paranoia is too tortured to go into here in detail. The immediate point is that Lieberman emerged from it a "loser" but also a more powerful and independent man than before he sought the vice presidency.

By 2008 the increasingly conservative senator had abandoned his party almost altogether. Although he continued to caucus with Senate Democrats, Lieberman got reelected as an independent in Connecticut. In December 2007, Lieberman endorsed McCain, emphasizing that the Arizona senator could reach across party lines to lead the nation. His endorsement was doubly valuable for McCain, whose campaign looked to be on the ropes at the time.

Anyone who knew the Senate and its composition as America entered the 2008 race knew that John McCain and Joe Lieberman were about as close as two colleagues could be. They were close before the December announcement, but after traveling the nation together campaigning for McCain's hopeless-turned-victorious effort to secure the nomination, the friendship only deepened.

As speculation over who McCain might pick as his vice presidential nominee grew during the late spring and into the summer, those closest to McCain more and more mentioned Lieberman as a consensus candidate who could offer something different to the nation—his Independent Party status and his devout Jewish faith—from an otherwise boring roster of potential candidates.

During the month or so leading up to the Republican convention, I had many a conversation with longtime former Republican colleagues and friends. By sheer coincidence I got a call from one of the most prominent longtime friends of the Bush family, a close acquaintance of both the first President Bush and the sitting President Bush. This person was not only close to family of the powerful Mercer Reynolds but had another interesting connection. He had served a prominent role in Mitt Romney's fundraising machine in the race for president.

We talked over who McCain might select as his running-mate. As I had become convinced that Romney's position on the GOP ticket had already been secured, I was not being disingenuous in throwing his name into the conversation.

This person with whom I spoke is a well-known national behind-the-scenes Bush-establishment Republican who has held titles and positions beyond imagination. Like so many in this tight-knit group, he is soft-spoken and careful in the choice of his words. But the mention of Romney lifted both his voice and his spirits. It was very clear that he, like others close to the Bush family, was pushing hard for a Romney nomination. He seemed buoyed by the growing likelihood that McCain would pick his man.

There was just one problem. John McCain had, for all intents and purposes, already picked his man. And it was a man.

Just weeks before the Republican convention in St. Paul, I received the strongest of background stories from a virtually unimpeachable source. John McCain had decided to choose Joe Lieberman as his running-mate. I was inclined to dismiss it, both in behind-the-scenes discussions and when asked about the issue on television. But again, my source was unimpeachable and would have been in a position to know exactly what was going on.

As the story goes, McCain, with just a matter of weeks to go before his nomination became official, gave Sen. Lieberman the impression that he would be McCain's man. In fact, so the story goes, he informed him that Lieberman would be the nominee. But when McCain revealed this to his own inner circle, he found himself under siege.

Why? Steve Kornacki of the *New York Observer* provides a plausible explanation: "But Mr. Rove and other prominent Republican establishment power players essentially sabotaged Mr. Lieberman—ostensibly because of his pro-choice views (and nominal ties to Senate Democrats), but really for a much different, more Machiavellian reason: They wanted Mr. Romney on the ticket."

Kornacki's article is a hypothetical, which he pieces together. And it's possible that my source could have been caught up in conjecture as well. But I doubt it. The Rove/Bush organization had been gently pushing McCain to pick Romney for months. And perhaps with good reason.

Romney had the looks, the brains, and the guts to fight an Obama-Biden ticket with real firepower. Would it have been to the benefit of Rove and Bush supporters if Romney had been on the

ticket? Sure. Had McCain-Romney won, the Republican establishment would have had the same situation they had with George H.
W. Bush as Ronald Reagan's vice president: one of their own in the
fold, and poised to take them back into the promised land.

And if McCain-Romney were to lose, then Romney would be
set to become the leading candidate for the GOP nomination in 2012.

Regardless of whether McCain's actions were misinter-
preted, or if instead he ran his preference for Lieberman by some of
those among the pro-Romney support base, this much seems plain:
He had led Romney to believe he was the likely nominee. The only
other names halfheartedly floated were ones like Minnesota Gov.
Tim Pawlenty and Florida Gov. Charlie Crist. I thought he should
have considered the seasoned Texas Sen. Kay Bailey Hutchison. But
as McCain led Romney on, some of the Republican establishment
money started to blow his way.

If my source's story and the conjecture of many beyond the
Observer's Kornacki are all even close to being true, some version of
this scenario would explain two things: Mitt Romney's initial reaction to not being selected by McCain, and the painful lack of vetting
of Sarah Palin, who seemed to have been selected at the last minute
as her party's vice presidential nominee.

In its online diary of the election known as "The Trail," the
Washington Post reported: "The Palin pick left bruised feelings among
the short list contenders. . . . Two senior Republican officials close to
Mitt Romney (and Tim Pawlenty) said they were both rudely strung
along and 'now feel manipulated. . . .They know they were used as
decoys well after McCain decided not to pick them'."

A subsequent article published just before the 2008 November vote further asserted that Lieberman had indeed been McCain's
choice up to the last days before the convention.

If all true, then the source of Alaska Gov. Sarah Palin as
the surprise late pick by John McCain would not only make sense,
it would be a classic McCain maneuver. Having led the GOP estab-

lishment along throughout the spring and summer, McCain and the party's bluebloods danced an uncomfortable but necessary dance. The establishment began to put together its first real fundraisers for their nominee-to-be. And McCain winked and back-slapped Mitt Romney as Romney, within a matter of days after leaving the presidential contest, sucked it up and went all out for McCain. Perhaps it could be labeled a belated "Nancy Reagan revenge."

How and why Palin became John McCain's choice for vice president might never be known. Ironically, a *New York Times* account of Palin's selection credits Schmidt and Davis with having reached the conclusion that Palin was the right choice for McCain. Regardless, neither Romney nor McCain would ever have a reason to admit that Romney was misled. And Lieberman would remain the loyal soldier for McCain to the bitter end. After all, he had no GOP power ladder upon which to climb.

One thing is for sure. The Palin selection was a swift one. So swift that the controversy and celebrity both hit at the exact same time, giving the McCain camp several days of heartburn, several weeks of afterglow, and then a lot to ponder.

It happened just after what most pundits judged a near perfect Democratic National Convention in Denver. With so little excitement waiting ahead for the GOP convention, which was to follow just a week after the Democrats, the coronation of Barack Obama was judged to have provided America's full complement of both fears and tears for the convention season.

First the tears. On the opening night of the convention an ailing Sen. Ted Kennedy addressed the convention. He belied the dire circumstances of his health with a passionate "Last Lion" speech to the convention hall. Ironically, the man he had overshadowed at the 1976 Democratic convention was once again left behind by circumstances and timing. Jimmy Carter's "address" to the convention was actually a short film of the former president followed by a brief appearance of President and Mrs. Carter on the stage—waving but not given a chance to speak.

Because of the role Kennedy had played in the Obama candidacy and the sadness over his malignant brain tumor, Kennedy was moved to the "A" spot of the night—speaking to thunderous applause and just before Michelle Obama.

The "fear" portion of the convention was the media hype over whether on one night Hillary and the next night Bill Clinton would throw their full verbal support behind Barack Obama. Hillary used her appearance as a means of demonstrating her remaining popularity, particularly with women. Those in the convention hall certainly loved her. She managed to leverage her unqualified support for Obama as a springboard in front of the entire convention to give her a well-deserved moment of glory.

The following night Bill Clinton spoke as only he can. He electrified the convention and reminded most viewers what it was like to see a real, live, and popular former Democratic president.

Vice presidential nominee Joe Biden followed with an acceptance speech that was more than adequate. The stage was set for the main event—Barack Obama's speech.

For that historic event, the convention was moved from the smaller convention hall to Denver's Invesco Field at Mile High Stadium. Over 75,000 people would fill the arena. Obama's detractors had caught wind of an elaborate staging that would include "Greek columns," giving the impression of the crowning of an emperor.

But when they appeared on television, the columns hardly looked overwhelming. In fact, the only thing that was overwhelming was the reaction and size of the crowd. As a stand-alone speech, Obama's acceptance oratory had its peaks and valleys. And like most acceptance speeches, it began to run too long. But towards the end, Obama started to pick up the cadence of the great African American ministers and civil rights leaders of the past. And he did it without appearing to be lapsing into some parody of Jesse Jackson or Al Sharpton.

Instead there was a hint of Martin Luther King, Jr., in his voice as he brought the crowd to its final moments of excitement. He had delivered as expected. And although the McCain campaign had, prior to the convention, struck with an early television commercial attempting to portray Obama and his favorable media attention as more befitting a "rock star" than a true leader of the free world, Obama somehow managed to keep a 75,000 person arena from casting him in that light. His polling numbers generally saw either a bounce or a tick upwards after what most called a nearly flawless gathering of the Democratic Party.

For John McCain, the timing of all this seemed to be against him, as it so often had since he announced his candidacy. Just as the Democrats concluded their convention and the Republicans readied for theirs, a major hurricane seemed poised to hit New Orleans. Recall that Hurricane Katrina's devastation of that city in 2005 had also devastated George W. Bush's presidency. The Federal government's response to Katrina had been almost universally condemned as inadequate. On top of the Iraq war, it may have driven the last nail into his political coffin.

The maverick candidate McCain quickly decided to postpone at least the first night of the GOP convention. The Republicans could not be viewed as "partying in the middle of another Katrina."

Besides, he had stunned Obama's team by yanking their candidate's great performance in Denver off the front pages by announcing that Gov. Sarah Palin of Alaska would be his running mate.

But "the next Katrina" veered away from New Orleans and diminished from catastrophic status. By late Monday, it no longer seemed a threat to the dignity of the Republican convention.

Instead there was another storm brewing. One that formed not in the warm waters of the Gulf of Mexico, but in the cyber-centers of the now politically powerful World Wide Web.

It took almost no time after Palin was announced as McCain's vice presidential pick for stories to begin appearing on the Internet, suggesting that the young baby she "supposedly" had delivered earlier in the year, a child diagnosed with Down Syndrome, was not that of Palin, but of her daughter Bristol.

Republicans at first dismissed the story as the lowest of blows by unscrupulous left-wingers. But the authors of the story had indeed found smoke. They had simply missed the real fire.

To quell the rumors, Palin put forth a rather shocking statement. Her daughter Bristol had in fact not delivered a baby—at least not yet.

On September 1, 2008, Governor Palin preemptively announced that her teenaged daughter would not only have a child but would marry the teenage father-to-be some time later in the year. The media extravaganza began.

Palin is a petite brunette. Her trademark glasses add a pert dimension to her looks. She is an example of real sex appeal in the business in which too many think they are but aren't. This sexy mom syndrome became a gravitational pull for so many perceived American cultural contradictions that it left most people dazed and confused. Except, that is, for Republicans. Most of them were in love.

She hunted moose but looked like the stereotypical former beauty queen. Her husband Todd worked as an oil field production operator and commercial fisherman. And he looked the part, too.

Within a day of the disclosures of Palin's daughter's pregnancy, public opinion had turned against the media and in favor of Palin. Suddenly the Republican convention that seemed likely to be a snoozer was anything but.

All eyes turned to Palin's acceptance speech. Expecting a weak and nervous performance, the press and pundits got the opposite. Palin, nicknamed "Sarah Barracuda" by her teammates on her high school basketball team, came out for her speech in a full-court press. She attacked the biased media and declared herself the ultimate hockey mom. Then she decried an out-of-control Congress that appropriated tons of money for things like the controversial "Bridge to Nowhere" in Alaska, which she said she had flatly rejected.

Suddenly the Republican convention hall in St. Paul didn't just come to life. It lit up with energy. Was this the answer to eight years of George W. Bush and a GOP congressional delegation that had lost all of its zest and zeal?

The choice of Palin suddenly seemed genius. And in many ways it was.

Her name first started surfacing in national Republican circles in the summer of 2007. A prominent group of conservatives went to Alaska on a promotional cruise for two conservative national magazines. They met with Palin and got the buzz going.

She was everything you could want if you were a Republican looking for someone who could promote old-school conservative values but who could still honorably rupture from the GOP establishment. In fact, she was more. In July 2007, Fred Barnes of the *Weekly Standard* wrote a story about Palin called, "The Most Popular Governor."

About a year later, *Weekly Standard* editor Bill Kristol, a former staffer with Dan Quayle, appeared on *Fox News Sunday* to predict that McCain would pick Palin as his running mate. And the conservative Kristol was not alone. My company's own Tom Baxter weighed in on the subject. And he had no conservative bias. He's generally considered to have a more liberal bent to his views, given his years circulating in the Cox media world. Baxter, in the spring of 2008, told CNN International viewers that he thought Palin would be McCain's pick.

Baxter was both surprised and amused when Palin was chosen by McCain. "It was just an on-the-spot reaction to an on-the-spot question," Tom laughs when recalling his educated guess. "I just had a hunch. I had read something about her and just thought . . . hmm."

It seemed everyone was thrilled with McCain's eleventh-hour choice of Sarah Palin, except for the Washington media—and the Bush/Romney establishment.

Unfortunately for John McCain, those were two powerful forces who would attempt to make him pay for being creative and independent in his thinking.

For several weeks after Governor Palin's choice, her star kept rising. So did McCain's. In mid-September, for the first time in months, he found himself leading in most all the "horse race" polls of the national popular vote. Soon enough, though, McCain's team would go into a tailspin, thanks to a combination of controllable events—such as media interviews with Palin—and uncontrollable events.

It was the uncontrollable variety that would take the dreaded, traditional "October Surprise" of campaigning infamy and convert it to a September one for McCain. For Palin and McCain, the brief days of glory would truly be fleeting.

On the upside, ravenous media overreaction to Palin's daughter's pregnancy appeared to turn the public against the press instead of against Palin. The incident seemed to boost her outsider status and magnify the defiance she had already displayed by picking a fight with "media elites."

But Palin would soon learn the many ways media has of slicing and dicing its detractors.

Even so, new events would soon far outdistance squabbling with the media as a blow to McCain and Palin. Call it conspiracy or fate or chance, but new happenings were about to hit Americans in the only place they take personally—their wallets.

★ 32 ★

"BURNING DOWN THE HOUSE"

February 7, 2008, was a day on the campaign trail, in Congress, and in the general news cycle that was flooded with the usual variety of reportage. But the biggest story of the day was hardly noticed. It would prove to be the first sign that the housing disaster I had first predicted in a newspaper column in March 2006 was, to paraphrase Rev. Jeremiah Wright, America's "chickens coming home to roost."

For years, investment banking firms on Wall Street had offered their well-heeled clients an alternative to money markets which, being "non-traditional banks," left them unable to offer certain "pedestrian products." Customers who sold out of stocks or bonds and who wanted to park their money while earning some reasonable rate of return had to be enticed to stay with the investment banks in some other capacity. That would turn out to be a financial vehicle known as the "Auction Rate Security." Ironically, according to sources, it was first introduced to investors by Goldman Sachs in 1988 after reportedly having been "invented" by an expert at another Wall Street firm in 1984—a firm called Lehman Brothers.

Auction Rate Securities, or ARSs, basically took debt instruments with long-term dates of maturity—say municipal bonds—and regularly reset that particular instrument's interest rate at private auctions. The auctions were typically held every 7, 28, or 35 days, with interest being paid at the end of the short period that the bond or other form of "paper" was held.

For decades these became Wall Street's highly competitive alternative to conventional money markets. Investors were told by brokers, who had no reason to believe otherwise, that the investment, when adjusted for the various non-taxable aspects of an ARS, was as safe as and stronger in return to the investor than traditional money markets. That is until February 7, when the auctions of these ARSs began to fail because investors declined to offer bids on them. Within weeks, the percentage of Auction Rate Security bids that failed to have participants had risen to eighty percent.

High-wealth clients and retired investors—those who relied on these Wall Street versions of money markets—found their cash frozen. Some firms went so far as to send out statements showing that the seemingly safe Auction Rate Securities their clients held had lost a highly discounted amount of their value. One institution showed the securities as having no value at all.

Because it impacted a relatively small segment of the public and because most on Wall Street felt certain that the stall in auctions was some temporary fluke, the sudden tie-up of liquidity and failure of a time-tested Wall Street investment tool went mostly unnoticed by elected officials, the presidential candidates, and the press.

That was all about to change. By early August, the New York attorney general made it clear that, one by one, investment firms that marketed these securities had misled their clients into believing that an Auction Rate Security was as safe as a money market account with a bank. Huge investment firms and the investment arms of major banks prepared to settle up with their clients. The first of the firms to offer to buy back their clients' securities at full value was Citigroup. That firm alone would shell out about $7.3 billion. And billions more would soon be promised to be repaid by a multitude of other firms that would soon be forced to enter into similar "agreements" with various regulatory authorities.

Throughout the early part of the 2008 campaign, John McCain admitted in response to specific questions about economic issues that his greatest area of expertise was not the economy. That confession was a mistake, of course. All the more because the experienced U.S. senator was probably underestimating his own knowledge and expertise.

The political damage of McCain's too-honest admission would soon be compounded by Lehman Brothers's file for bankruptcy. This was the same investment bank credited with inventing the somewhat obscure Auction Rate Security.

I could hardly believe my ears when McCain, speaking in the city where my nationally syndicated newspaper column is based, Jacksonville, Florida, said, "I think, still, the fundamentals of our economy are strong."

Just the previous week, both the Federal National Mortgage Association (Fannie Mae) and the Federal Home Loan Mortgage Association Corporation (Freddie Mac) had been placed under conservatorship by the Federal government. Both entities were bleeding to death over sub-prime loans that simply couldn't be paid back.

As McCain spoke, the Dow Jones index was headed for its biggest tumble since the day the markets reopened after 9/11. And the situation would only continue to get worse. Suddenly financial institutions were folding like cheap tents. The stock market would soon start bouncing from dramatic highs to record lows with accumulating signs that the bottom was dropping out.

If McCain had one week that was worse than any other, it was the one following the Lehman Brothers's bankruptcy, which triggered an ensuing string of financial disasters.

Few ever realized that later in that week, liquidity for money market funds, a financial vehicle known to virtually all American investors, froze up. That forced the Treasury Department to issue temporary insurance for money market deposits. Large corporations were privately told by government officials that the lack of confidence in the banking system had led to a near freeze on both credit and the availability of cash. Otherwise strong corporations would likely find it hard to find their financial institutions capable of covering expenses such as payroll. The situation was desperate.

For those given to even modest bouts of paranoia, the rapidly unfolding events of September 2008 were giving rise to any number of questions and concerns. Why had a clearly growing housing market crisis suddenly come to reach its final meltdown with just a month-and-a-half to go before a presidential election? Why, in the following weeks, would positive moves by the Federal Reserve or Treasury Department—efforts that would serve to prop up ailing institutions and provide additional protection result, not in a calmer stock market, but a more volatile one, one that would often see in the last thirty minutes of a day's trading a massive sell-off that left no chance of recovery that day? The result of the latter phenomenon was, of course, a sell-off in foreign markets that were spooked by massive declines in the United States.

Such questions could only be asked rhetorically at the time. There was no time for anything else. The nation's economy was only days away from collapse. Insiders say that following a complete briefing of the situation, President Bush told one intimate that hearing about the sudden crisis was as shocking as when he was told of the planes hitting the World Trade Center towers.

By the end of the week Treasury Secretary Henry Paulson and Federal Reserve Chairman Ben Bernanke cobbled together legislation that would allow the government, with almost complete discretion given to Paulson, to buy back troubled assets from financial institutions across the nation.

The following week, it seemed that Congress was moving towards approval of the proposed legislation. Both Sen. McCain and Sen. Obama had agreed that the legislation was necessary.

Other big players disagreed. Chief among them was, of all people, Newt Gingrich. Once again he would reach into the reserves of knowledge and power he retained from his days as House Speaker, this time to shape an aspect of the 2008 race. He had already done so once with his "Drill Here, Drill Now" public relations campaign. In essence, it had forced McCain to adopt a strong position on rescinding Federal legislation that prohibits drilling for oil and natural gas in various American locations. Gingrich forced the issue in the late spring and early summer as gas prices topped well over four dollars a gallon in many parts of the nation.

But this time Newt's role would be less obvious—and maybe more significant. It was no secret among GOP members that Newt was telling them that the proposed financial "bailout" was a terrible bill and could lead to unfettered executive branch powers if passed. As it was originally proposed, the bill might have been as bad as Gingrich said. On September 23, with the vote on the bill looming, Gingrich declared that McCain needed to oppose it because it was a "dead loser" on Election Day.

Suddenly McCain was under assault from all sides. He had committed to bipartisan support for the "emergency rescue" bill. Yet Gingrich and his loyal former colleagues in the House were building up quite the head of steam in opposition to the legislation.

Making things more difficult for McCain was his camp's decision about the first presidential debate. It was scheduled for September 26, or just three days after the vote on the bailout bill. The subject of the debate was to be foreign affairs, McCain's strength. It was to be held in Oxford, Mississippi, and moderated by *PBS News-Hour*'s Jim Lehrer.

McCain's people realized that with the entire world watching the U.S. economic meltdown, the debate would inevitably move into the territory of Obama's perceived strength, the economy (if in the context of worldwide financial affairs).

McCain suspended his campaign and flew to Washington, supposedly to work on the bailout legislation. His campaign suggested that the debate be postponed and even said that McCain might skip the debate altogether, given the gravity of the financial situation.

The Obama camp realized the political gift that had landed in their laps. They countered McCain's posturings by saying that the president and Congress seemed to have things under control. They said Obama would take any actions he needed to, but that he felt no need to suspend his campaign or skip the debate.

Suddenly the so-called bailout bill became John McCain's legislation. The maverick senator was now trapped in a situation that had few, if any, positive outcomes possible for him. After a ballyhooed "bipartisan meeting" of congressional leaders at the White House broke down—mainly due to McCain's and Obama's joint presence there—the stage was set for the legislation to crash and burn.

Soon enough McCain had his decision made for him: The Democratic leadership that controlled both the House and Senate gave reassurances that a vote would be taken the following week and that the bill would pass. McCain would be going to Mississippi.

★ 33 ★

MISSISSIPPI BURNING

Haley Barbour is nobody's fool. The Republican Mississippi governor is a lifetime pro at running political campaigns, moving legislation in Washington, D.C., running traps for Republican national politics, and generally getting exactly what he wants. And he really wanted the debate in Oxford to happen as scheduled on September 26. He wasn't going to let McCain spoil one of the biggest events to occur in his state in decades. "There won't be a damn light on in the House or Senate Friday night," he reportedly told McCain aides. "You guys are gonna look like fools. Meanwhile they'll have him [Barack Obama] on the air and you guys with an empty podium. . . .They are gonna ask, 'What could John McCain be doing that's so important back in Washington on a Friday evening and with everybody having gone home?" Haley was right, and he also knew exactly how to apply the pressure at the right time.

The debate was more than a debate. It was a celebration for Mississippi and its pride and joy, the University of Mississippi, still affectionately known as Ole Miss. In the early 1960s, the school had been the site of one of the ugliest chapters in modern American history, the attempt to enroll the University's first black student, James Meredith, and the ensuing violence that erupted over his enrollment.

But now there was a new, vibrant Mississippi, and the state's Republican governor was determined to show the world just how far his state had advanced. McCain was coming to that debate, or he would incur the wrath of Haley Barbour and a considerable network of Republican movers and shakers.

McCain did himself a favor and came debating. Our firm conducted another post-debate national survey, much like the one we had taken immediately after the CNN/YouTube debate of the Republicans nearly a year earlier in Florida. That was the one that confirmed that former Arkansas Gov. Mike Huckabee had won the contest; that debate and poll essentially chopped the legs out from under candidates such as Mitt Romney, Fred Thompson, and Rudy Giuliani.

Both in Florida and now in Mississippi, our polls were fundamentally different from other "instant" surveys polling the debate outcomes. The difference was simple: We not only gathered the results from a random national sample of genuinely undecided voters, but we also took the time to scientifically "weight" the results. That meant that if many more respondents were Democrats than Republicans, or perhaps if many more men than women responded, adjustments could be made so that the numbers would accurately reflect the demographic makeup of the national electorate.

To be candid, all three presidential debates were boring. I was surprised that McCain held his own in the Mississippi one, given that he had spent most of the week embroiled in inextricably linking himself with the divisive battle in Congress over the looming bailout bill.

The McCain team had been right about this: The nominal foreign-policy debate quickly morphed into one that was at least partly about the economy. This was territory less comforting to McCain.

Asked to score the debate for a news organization, I viewed the contest a tie. Most in the newsroom where I was viewing the contest felt about the same. So we were shocked when we listened to the major broadcast networks all declaring that Obama had scored a big win.

"Well," I said, "we will know when our poll comes in." We were polling for the newspaper *Memphis Commercial Appeal*, which is the paper of record for the region where the debate was being held. Our survey seemed in line with my expectations. Of the undecided voters polled, forty-two percent said Obama won, forty-one said McCain, and seventeen couldn't make up their minds.

Then I heard the results of a CBS News poll that showed Obama winning the debate handily. Trust me on this, because as a former national debate champion who started out in politics teaching candidates how to debate, I know a lopsided contest when I see one. For example, the second debate, a town-hall format that was held in St. Louis, was a rambling wreck of a performance by McCain. It was so bad by the Republican that I didn't need a poll to know he had lost.

But something seemed fishy about this CBS survey of the first debate and, once again, it was. CBS had teamed up with a company that claimed to have created a statistically valid group of participants who would evaluate the debate. There was just one problem. They were using the Internet.

How many seventy-year-olds do you know who routinely surf the Web? Sure, there are some, but our studies indicate that they are less than a representative sample of the actual bloc of voters that make up the sixty-five-and-over crowd. And as a group at that time, these were the voters generally moving in McCain's direction.

When the poll was reported, no one bothered to explain that it was an Internet response survey. Had this been known, I doubt the CBS poll would have been so widely relied upon. Then again, very little surprised me in the last months leading up to the election.

Ironically, I was seated next to former CBS anchor and host of *Face the Nation*, Bob Schieffer, two days later at a luncheon. It was

Monday, and the House of Representatives was preparing to vote on the emergency bailout bill that both McCain and Obama had endorsed. While there were a few rumblings in the media, most reports that morning suggested that the bill would pass.

Schieffer is one of the nicest people in national media. He's also experienced and a real pro. I told him that I thought Newt Gingrich had been hard at work behind the scenes with his old colleagues, trying to kill the bill. "You know," he said, "I hadn't heard that, but for some reason, I really don't think it's going to pass. They just don't have the votes."

After Schieffer spoke, we were all headed out when a group of stunned men watching a television set in a nearby lounge area pulled me aside and pointed to the screen. It was C-SPAN. The clock indicating the remaining time on the bailout vote read 0:00. The bill had failed.

"Can't they do something?" one man asked me, sweat beading on his forehead. "Don't they have extra time or something? The Dow [Jones] is crashing. These idiots!"

Bob Schieffer had been right, as I had. NBC's Andrea Mitchell later reported that Gingrich had played a heavy hand in lobbying House members to kill the original version of the bill. I certainly didn't need to email or call him to confirm Mitchell's story. I had felt it in my gut and knew as soon as Newt had issued his edict that McCain could not win if he voted for the bill. Once again, Newt was having a big, if largely unacknowledged, impact on the presidential race.

The defeat of the bill in the House forced the administration to bargain again with the House and Senate in a desperate effort to get something in place before the financial system, especially the credit markets, ground to a halt. The whole thing proved to be the biggest single momentum shift in the 2008 election. After that vote, McCain would never again lead in any of the many national polls of the presidential race. Suddenly, like the stock market, John McCain's campaign was tail-spinning.

PART SEVEN

FEAR FACTORS

★ 34 ★

CURIOUS TIMING

By the time the Senate passed a new version of the misnamed financial "bailout" bill and the House came around to approving it as well, America was nearing panic. By early-to-mid-October, the world was, too.

Polling showed that Americans felt Barack Obama was better prepared to deal with economic issues, although why was unclear. Probably it was enough for many that Obama was a sort of anti-George W. Bush. John McCain wasn't Bush either, but he was having a hard time persuading voters that he wasn't tainted with the sour scent of the Republican president.

As has been noted throughout this book, the timing of chaotic and even tragic events in 2008 often seemed beyond coincidence, enough to raise suspicions even among those who normally blanch at words like "conspiracy" or "manipulation." But the last weeks of the campaign would be awash with both spoken and unspoken theories of plots, past associations, and potential fraud.

One thing did seem particularly odd to me, and I first wrote about it in August 2007 in my nationally syndicated column:

"The stock market is now artificially supported by infusions of Federal cash printed so rapidly that the ink hasn't dried.

"As we all know, the dollar has been falling rapidly. News this week that China, which holds a massive amount of our currency, will be 'divesting itself' of the dollar over time has sent shivers of fear through the financial world.

"Two weeks ago, I sold every stick of stock I own. That's only the second time I've done that. The last time was in the spring of 2000. I think you can remember what followed—the Internet crash.

"I'm not pretending to be an economist, though I sometimes 'play' one on TV. But when you are polling all across the nation every day and you get data back saying that people feel burdened by debt, or that people in high growth areas are scared to death that their house value is plummeting, then you don't have to be Milton Friedman to know something is not right.

"As my friend and one-time worthy opponent James Carville put it back in 1992, 'It's the economy, stupid.'

"And what's amazing is that, based on the polls I've seen, the American people realized it long before the financial analysts or the politicians did.

"Now we have presidential candidates still making immigration their huge issue—and it is important—while the entire underpinnings of our economy could be washed away.

"This is a rapidly developing storm, one that some of us could see coming . . . ."

If I could see the disaster that awaited our nation and the world just a year or so prior to the great financial collapse of 2008, surely there were many brighter minds with much greater wealth who understood the significant crisis we would all soon be facing.

The essential question in this context is why did the obvious become obvious with just two months to go in perhaps the most historic presidential race in modern times? When the Auction Rate Securities market began to fail early in 2008, alarm bells should have been going off in every campaign of every presidential candidate left standing. But they didn't.

After the meltdown of the stock markets in late September and early October, former presidential candidate Mike Huckabee had an interesting suggestion while appearing on FOX News. The former Arkansas governor said, "In the last 12 days, every single day, in the half hour before trading ends, there has been an unusual flurry of activity; nine-fold from what is normal.

"If a person was going to manipulate the marketplace and create, in essence, a collapse and a calamity, this could have as great an impact as any type of bomb that would ever be set off. It affects the entire world. What 9/11 did was affect the economy, though it affected human lives first and foremost. But this kind of act, if in fact there is something going on here, could be that bad actors are manipulating the marketplace with computerized trades using late-in-the-day activity to create a panic; and because it happened so late, the market can't react to it, and then the media talks about how terrible things are, and that just further escalates the problem."

Was Huckabee paranoid? Was he advancing fantastic conspiracy theories? Or could there be something to his observations?

Apparently Federal officials felt there were questions to be answered. On October 20, Bloomberg News reported that U.S. regulators had begun investigating whether investors manipulated end-of-day stock prices so that the Dow Jones Industrial Average would swing, often violently, in the last few minutes of trading in the days of late September and into October of 2008.

The same day, the *Washington Post* reported that the Securities and Exchange Commission was looking into possible manipulation of the massive credit swaps market.

But the most telling insight on all this may have come in a *Wall Street Journal* article of September 30. Manhattan (New York)

Dist. Atty. Robert Morgenthau wrote, "The $700 billion in Treasury Secretary Henry Paulson's current proposed rescue plan pales in comparison to the volume of dollars that now escapes the watchful eye, not only of the U.S. regulators, but of the media and the general public as well.

"There is $1.9 trillion, almost all of it run out of the New York metropolitan area, that sits in the Cayman Islands, a secrecy jurisdiction. Another $1.5 trillion is lodged in four other secrecy jurisdictions . . . [all] outside the safety net—beyond the reach of U.S. regulators."

An overlay of many complicating factors by October 2008 was contributing to what was now being called "the global financial crisis." That made the sudden onset of the situation, and the how and why of it, almost impossible to decipher.

For McCain and the Republicans, the daily barrage of bad economic news was taking a serious toll. Now McCain was starting to trail Obama in toss-up states that were once realistically coveted by the Republicans. Minnesota was one. Hardly a month before, it had hosted the GOP convention. In the South, Florida, North Carolina, and even Georgia suddenly seemed within Obama's reach. And the Republicans' usually reliable state of Virginia was witnessing polls that showed Obama likely heading to a big win. Out West, GOP safe-haven states like Colorado and Nevada were leaning Obama's way.

During all this, conservative-oriented talk show hosts were offering a grab bag of advice to the McCain campaign. Most of it amounted to suggested issues that could serve as bellwether campaign themes.

FOX News host and nationally syndicated radio star Sean Hannity spent weeks detailing the rise of Obama in intricate detail. Hannity raised serious questions about Obama's years as a "community organizer" in Chicago and about his association with the Association of Community Organizations for Reform, or ACORN.

Debate raged over the exact extent of Obama's relationship with the group. Evidence surfaced that he had served as an attorney for a firm representing ACORN and other clients, who sued the state of Illinois in the 1990s to enforce the state's "motor voter" registration program.

Allegations were made that, early in his career, Obama had taught community organizer classes for ACORN as part of an effort to force lending institutions to make what would later prove to be the same "risky" home loans that caused the financial disintegration of 2008. And it appeared that the Obama campaign had paid an organization that sub-contracted with ACORN for some services during the 2008 election cycle, although the exact amount was fuzzy, and the Obama camp claimed that it was for the rental of lights and other equipment for a rally.

But what made ACORN prominently controversial in 2008 was that its vast voter registration effort, which was indisputably to Obama's benefit, had turned into, at least, a public relations disaster by late October. John Fund reporting in the *Wall Street Journal* wrote that the group's leader had by this time admitted that 400,000 of the 1.3 million new voters the organization had signed up for the 2008 cycle had been determined to be either duplicate names or fraudulent.

But the McCain campaign chose to merely flirt with the ACORN issue with Web advertisements and other occasional references to its operations. By late October, many voters still didn't fully understand ACORN, any connection it might have to Obama or an effort to elect Obama, or any of the potential problems it faced, including allegations of tax violations.

Sean Hannity also kept pushing on the relationship between Obama and William "Bill" Ayers. That's the man who was the founder of the Weather Underground, a group that carried out the bombing in the 1960s and 1970s of public buildings as a way to protest the Vietnam War. The Pentagon and the U.S. Capitol building were among its targets.

Again, the extent of Obama's relationship with anyone or anything compromising was hard to pin down. Hannity seemed able to document that Ayers had held a meet-and-greet in his home for Obama when Obama was seeking his seat in the Illinois state Senate. Also, Obama and Ayers had served on the board of a civic organization charged with distributing scholarships in the Chicago area. It was clear that the two knew each another, but Obama denied that he had any regular or recent conversations with Ayers and said that Ayers had not endorsed him for president.

I first started listening to talk radio in high school. Back then, I would often drift off to sleep listening to a rock station with my bulky headphones on. One night I tuned into the local AM news station and heard the voice of a man interviewing a prominent newswoman who had covered many presidents in her career. The interview fascinated me, as did the man who seemed to be asking all the right questions. The show was broadcast on the Mutual Radio Network, and the man's name was Larry King. Who could know that, years later, King would become an international star, and be on television?

Sean Hannity gained his entry into television as a fast-rising talk radio host in the early-to-mid-1990s. I had come to know Sean during his stint in Atlanta, just before he left to host New York radio and later become one of the biggest stars of our time in radio and television.

Hannity seemed more passionate than McCain himself about pressing the issues of ACORN and Ayers on a sustained basis, so much so that Obama began to reference Hannity on the campaign trail. Hannity had managed to do what McCain seemed unable to accomplish—to get under Obama's skin.

Hannity's colleague at FOX was, of course, the star of cable and radio, Bill O'Reilly. He literally chased Obama across the campaign trail, trying to get the senator to talk to him on camera. O'Reilly often seems to have a slight twinkle in his eye, as if to say, "I'm tough, but I'm not mean. And I really know that this stuff is all fun."

O'Reilly finally got his interview with Obama in early September. He grilled Obama on issues such as his failure to support the so-called surge of additional troops in Iraq, an American strategic move generally considered to have been successful. But true to O'Reilly's style, each time he put Obama on the ropes, he gently pulled back in an effort to get more out of the interview. His tactic worked: The interview earned a huge viewership and even skated clear of the customary attacks on FOX News's personalities that other media usually engage in.

From Rush Limbaugh, the godfather of conservative talk radio, to nationally syndicated stars such as Libertarian Neal Boortz, there was no shortage of arguments and arguers against Obama. Limbaugh implored McCain to attack Obama on his plans for the economy and to verbally slug Obama rather than jab at him. Boortz covered a batch of topics, from ACORN to Obama's tax plan, which he said would destroy any incentive for small business to grow—or even exist.

If the talk masters could be believed, John McCain had everything he needed to knock Obama to the ground. There was just one problem: Barack Obama was not even feeling a glancing blow.

Worse for McCain, for the first time since cable news had become many people's primary source of news, there was in this presidential cycle strong, unvarnished, and left-leaning counter-programming. The most virulent and effective of these shows was MSNBC's *Countdown with Keith Olbermann*. Olbermann had once been a prominent sports anchor at ESPN.

By September 2008, MSNBC had relieved both Olbermann and longtime political host Chris Matthews from their roles as anchors of the headline campaign news shows because of their perceived biases. To me, the situation seemed a bit unfair. Olbermann knew he was biased. The whole idea was for him to be an antidote to the believed far-right programming at FOX. His "Countdown" of the daily news stories had morphed into a list of mistakes and mischieviousness on the part of conservatives, in this case McCain and Sarah Palin.

Unlike Olbermann, Chris Matthews had worked in high inner circles of the political arena. Granted, his experience was mostly with Democrats. But he knew the political scene and took great pride in being seen as objective.

Olbermann's partisan tack had worked for him. His ratings grew, although not enough to catch O' Reilly in the same time slot. But Matthews apparently got the hook right when his savvy and encyclopedic political knowledge were most needed, all the more after the sudden death of Tim Russert, who was easily NBC's all-star political go-to guy.

I had appeared on Matthews's show in the past. While I knew firsthand that he can be tough—and tough to keep up with, what with his hockey-announcer verbal speed—I respected him as an expert. I can still remember seeing him in Washington, walking with former U.S. House Speaker Tip O'Neil, during my days as a lowly adviser to Newt Gingrich and Georgia U.S. Sen. Mack Mattingly.

I never could have imagined then that it would be me standing next to a Speaker of the House in the same halls of Congress just a decade or so later. It amounts to this: I have great respect for political talking heads who have actually "worn the pads" on the political playing field—as had both Matthews and Russert.

Throughout October it seemed that, regardless of what various media superstars had to write or say, John McCain could not stitch together a whole cloth of coherence for his campaign message. The daily spate of bad news about international financial markets was also accumulating bad news for him. Fears of joblessness and recession in the United States were rampant.

It was about now that our firm started a relationship with the hot political print and Web news organization Politico. We started with them with the novel concept of polling "swing counties" in battleground states. That provided a better idea of the particulars of how voters in key states were thinking. We tracked these regions to test for movements up or down by the candidates. Then we polled the entire states in which these counties were found. It soon became clear that neither the counties nor the states were budging. Barack Obama was either carrying these battleground states or was close to the lead.

What the polls didn't measure was the massive ground operation that Obama's team had built across the nation. Using adapted versions of the same "community organizing" techniques Obama had taught years earlier, his team was burying the Republicans with an army of volunteers. He had many more campaign offices in competitive states. He also had a lot more money than McCain. For every television ad McCain ran, Obama ran three.

By the time early voting opened in the first set of states where it was allowed, a virtual sea of humanity appeared at the early polling locations. Police were brought in to direct unexpected traffic. Lines at early polling places were hours long, often twisting through corridors and spilling out into longer lines on the streets. And the early votes were going heavily for Obama.

Allegations of fraudulent voter registration flew all over the place. By late October, the Bush Justice Department announced that it would investigate allegations that as many as 200,000 voters were illegally on the voting rolls in that critical battleground state of Ohio. The paranoia grew intense. Republicans were convinced that millions of new voters were fraudulent. One obviously fake registration in Florida was under the name of one Mickey Mouse.

Democrats feared a last-minute effort by the Federal government to purge voting rolls and somehow contest states that the Democrats felt were otherwise likely to fall their way.

Would history repeat itself? Would allegations of voter fraud or tampering with the system cast its shadow on another American presidential contest, as it did in 2000?

This much was certain: In another sense, history was indeed repeating. To illustrate that point, one needed to look no further than Sen. McCain's choice of a vice-presidential running mate, Sarah Palin.

★ 35 ★

QUAYLIN PALIN

Once the Republican and Democratic presidential tickets were cemented, public opinion surveys eventually showed two things. First, that more people than not preferred Obama-Biden over McCain-Palin. Second, that voters overall believed that media had been most sympathetic to the Democrats. Nothing proved the case like media attention to Sarah Palin. Her treatment was not just figuratively, but sometimes literally comic.

For most Americans, NBC's *Saturday Night Live* has been a television icon that has helped the nation mark the years through its continuing assortment of political caricatures during presidential campaigns. There was Chevy Chase's version of a bumbling Gerald Ford, in which Chase made no attempt to try to look like the president. There was Dana Carvey's dead-on impersonation of George H. W. Bush. And don't forget the late Phil Hartman's uncanny rendition of Bill Clinton.

In the decade leading up to the 2008 race, *Saturday Night Live* and its political "commentary" prompted less and less water cooler comment on Monday mornings across the land. That all changed with Sarah Palin.

Former *SNL* star Tina Fey had gone on to star in a network comedy parody of behind-the-scenes goings-on at an *SNL*-like show. Now she was the deadest of ringers for the Alaska governor. From the Palin hair to the glasses to the vice presidential nominee's accent and "Joe Sixpack" lingo, Fey topped them all with her appearances as Palin.

The problem was that much "serious" media was also trying to make a caricature of Palin. Countless articles and reports questioned her experience and her suitability to take over as president if an elected McCain were to die or become disabled in office. She was also under attack for having allegedly forced Alaska's public safety commissioner out after he allegedly resisted pressure from Palin's husband, Todd, and others to dismiss a state trooper who was divorced from Palin's sister. Prior to this new, intense media scrutiny, allegations of misconduct by the trooper while off the job, plus an allegation that he used a taser on his child, all went largely unreported, or at least were never made clear to the public. The net of all this was that the serious ridicule and the comic ridicule converged to create a downward spiral in Palin's approval ratings.

And yes, history was repeating itself.

I first knew of former Vice President Dan Quayle from his early days in the same freshman class in the U.S. Senate as my then-boss and lifelong friend Mack Mattingly. Mattingly, who represented Georgia, had grown up in Quayle's home state of Indiana. I would come to know Quayle better and better as the years passed.

Of all of the political figures I ever came to know, the most opposite of his public persona was Dan Quayle. He is one of the brightest, most engaging, most self-effacing, and funniest people ever to serve in high office. When I tell this to my friends in journalism and to those who are new to politics, they are amazed. But it's true.

So how did Dan Quayle as George H. W. Bush's vice president end up with the image of a confused, timid half-wit who could

not even spell potato? Well, the easy answer would be the usual—
"the media." But that's not really the root of the story.

The real answer can be found in the brutal manner in which
Quayle—also a last-minute shock choice for vice president—was
manhandled by a furious Bush political operation that felt he had
bungled what now look like silly questions about the extent of his
military service.

Like Palin, Quayle was bashed for his perceived inexperi-
ence. In fact, the Bush team suddenly felt they had stumbled into
making a terrible selection with Quayle. What's little remembered
is that Bush trailed in the polls before the New Orleans Republican Convention in 1988 but took the lead and went on to win after
choosing Quayle.

But Quayle never really recovered politically from the
tongue-lashing and "handling" he got from the Bush campaign after
he landed on the ticket. To add insult to injury, during the Bush-
Quayle reelection effort in 1992, a comment about a then-popular
sitcom character—a left-leaning network talk anchor named "Mur-
phy Brown" who was portrayed by actress Candice Bergen—became
another moment of twisted mistreatment of Quayle. He had made a
comment about the show's main character, Brown, purposely choosing to become pregnant with the intent of being an unwed mother.
He suggested that it sent the wrong message to young women.

The comedy show struck back, ending an episode with
scores of "single family" parents saying how great their families were
. . . and likely so. But included among these real life families were
parents who were divorced or whose spouses had died. It made it
appear that Dan Quayle was attacking every one-parent family. It
was a gross distortion.

By the time the McCain-Palin team reached the end of
October, they realized that Palin was being "Dan Quayled" by the
Republican establishment. She openly rebelled against her "Bush

handlers," specifically a former aide to George W. Bush who Palin temporarily banned from her campaign airplane. Politico broke the story of Palin's belief that she had been led in the wrong direction by her handlers. She was right.

Not only had Palin been kept away from the media after the convention, but when she was finally put before the cameras in a big way, that, too, was a mistake. She subjected herself to long, in-depth interviews with two of the nation's top news anchors, ABC's Charlie Gibson and CBS's Katie Couric. She was ill-prepared for both. To make things worse, the McCain campaign decided that her Alaskan sense of style wasn't chic enough and went on a $150,000 spending spree to spruce her up—on the campaign's dime. When Politico broke that story as well, Palin was humiliated.

I had little doubt that Palin had likely been told of the saga of Dan Quayle—and likely from sources close to Quayle himself.

But even as she was being called a "diva" by some McCain intimates, and even though she sometimes seemed to wander off the vanilla script the campaign supplied her, the conservative base of the GOP was nevertheless falling madly in political love with her. The conservatives who saw Palin as the future of the new conservative movement weren't going to let her be the "fall person" should the McCain "express" end up in a train wreck.

In her debate with Joe Biden, Palin more than held her own but was immediately judged the loser by most of the networks and more of the so-called instant polls. But Sarah Palin was a fighter. She drew huge crowds on the campaign trail. And by the final weekend before the election, she had sought to soothe over any apparent break with the McCain camp and even with the so-called "Bush" handlers whom she had criticized. For Sarah Palin there was a future—with or without John McCain.

★ 36 ★

"JOE THE PLUMBER"
AND SPREADING THE WEALTH

On October 11, 2008, Samuel Joseph Wurzelbacher was playing football in his yard with his family. Barack Obama was stumping for votes in his Ohio neighborhood, and Wurzelbacher got the chance to ask Obama a question. "I am getting ready to buy a company that makes $250,000-$280,000 a year. Your new tax plan's going to tax me more, isn't it?"

Obama's full answer, which included several arguments as to how his plan would actually benefit Wurzelbacher's plumbing company and the plumber himself, never made it to air. Instead, one line became the centerpiece of the story. Obama said, as part of his lengthy answer, "I think you spread the wealth around and it's good for everybody." And thus began the more than fifteen minutes of fame for Joe Wurzelbacher—forever more to be dubbed "Joe the Plumber."

Within a day "Joe" was a household name, and Obama's answer seemed to be the smoking gun that indicated that an Obama administration would bring socialism to America. It's true that Obama arguably had one of the Senate's most liberal voting records. And his policies certainly targeted "families" with incomes of over $250,000 a year. Nonetheless, even he had to have been stunned that just one sentence in a detailed answer was being used to confirm him as a socialist candidate.

Joe the Plumber made a point bigger than he had imagined. Many in America indeed believed that the Obama ticket, combined with a Democratically controlled Congress, would bring about policies that would in fact amount to a significant redistribution of wealth. At any time in any other campaign for the presidency in modern times, being pigeonholed by even a minority of the population as an avowed redistributor of wealth would have spelled doom for a candidate.

But Obama's comment came at the same time that many Americans were pointing angrily to greedy CEOs and Wall Street executives. These everyday people weren't feeling particularly wealthy. And so, the term "spreading the wealth," once a code phrase that even the most liberal of politicians would avoid at any cost, wasn't getting much traction with the electorate as a term that would strike fear in their hearts.

But that didn't keep Joe the Plumber from becoming the focus of the final presidential debate, or the topic of McCain-Palin stump speeches. And when the McCain camp wasn't talking about Joe, Joe was busy talking to anyone with a camera and a microphone.

Our polling for Politico showed that McCain fared stronger in his final debate performance, moderated brilliantly by Bob Schieffer. (Our scientifically weighted post-debate poll showed the debate to be basically a tie.) And Joe the Plumber figured significantly in McCain's effort to illustrate how significantly Obama had broken with traditional political vocabulary on things like tax increases.

Joe the Plumber would, over the next few weeks, become the most unlikely of "team mascots" in modern political history. And it would truly be an election created for the history books. As early voting continued in states where it was allowed, the turnout was simply overwhelming. Long lines and allegations of machine malfunctions and incorrect ballots were being made in virtually every state. It was clear that voters were going to come charging to the polls like never before. Now a whole new set of problems were starting to come into play. It appeared that the American electoral system was literally unprepared for the crush of voters at polling places from coast-to-coast. This might be a clog so massive that even a plumber couldn't fix it.

★ 37 ★

WHERE'S JOE?

For Barack Obama, it was becoming clear that all he needed to do was to play the political version of prevent defense to win the presidency. In its final week, the McCain campaign had waved off any effort to revive mention of Obama's former pastor, Jeremiah Wright—despite that an independent conservative group had scraped together money for a decent television buy featuring Wright's outrageous past comments.

For the McCain team it was clear that Obama's comments to Joe the Plumber had opened the door to a much broader theme that Obama would advance a socialistic agenda that would pilfer concepts from past communist nations that could threaten capitalism and free speech.

I spoke to one of my closest friends in the world of high-end national GOP politics just a week prior to the election. He told me, "The [the McCain team] may have really found something here. . . . I mean the whole history of what a 'community organizer' really means, plus this guy's views of income redistribution. It all fits into a pretty scary scenario." He continued, "The problem is that they've waited too long to do anything with it. If you're going to call a man a socialist, a damn near Marxist, the first thing you have to do is explain to about half of America what those words mean and why they are so bad. But McCain has run out of time and money necessary to get that going."

With just five days to go and McCain desperately trying to defend traditionally Republican or other must-win states, Joe the Plumber was mentioned in virtually every stump speech by McCain.

Appearing in Defiance, Ohio, a state McCain had to carry to have any chance against Obama, McCain started in about Joe the Plumber. But the people in charge of arranging for Joe to be there forgot one thing about plumbers—they only give you a range of hours when they might make an appearance!

"Joe's with us today," said McCain. "Where is Joe? Is Joe with us today? Joe, I thought you were here today" McCain and his wife Cindy, dressed in windbreakers fighting the cool weather, looked desperately around the audience. But there was no Joe. He was a no-show. McCain, always quick on his feet, declared everyone in the crowd to be "Joes today. Everybody stand up."

I've been a part of campaigns where scheduling snafus and missed details in the last week start to pile up. They are clear signs that the wheels are coming off the campaign express.

Joe did manage to show at later events. But as NBC's *Nightly News* anchor Brian Williams appropriately noted during an appearance on a PBS program the night before the election, "Look how our attention was able to get pulled into pigs and lipstick and plumbers. We've got a plumber who is the third member of the GOP ticket, in effect." Williams was dead right.

Despite my desire to remain neutral in the race, two feelings were developing simultaneously in my gut. First, I felt truly sorry for John McCain. This man who had survived beatings and cruelty in a POW camp, who at age seventy-two had more energy than most thirty-five year olds, and who was a good and decent man, was being destroyed by the remnants of the party I had once helped, in my small way, build. The GOP establishment was either collapsing under the weight of consultants and strategists who had grown stale, or was playing stall-ball to see a good man and a devoted wife suffer, with no real zeal to push him to victory.

My gut told me it was the latter. It led me to write the following column, one which, ironically, received huge positive response from—of all groups, Republicans.

In my national column dated October 23, 2008, I wrote:

"I have seen this happen once or twice: a complete meltdown. It starts as an uphill year looking tougher by the day. It ends like a load of bricks falling on the GOP's head.

"There's one word that describes the reason for the rubble that likely will be on the Republicans' heads come Nov. 4—arrogance.

"The fish rots from the head. And I'm not talking about the well-intentioned John McCain, this year's winner of the 'Bob Dole Sacrificial Lamb' award.

"Instead, I mean President Bush, and, more importantly, those who served his administration by cajoling, misleading, and betraying him. They transformed him into what came to look like a cocky buffoon. They encouraged a good man to self-destruct.

"Now Bush has been abandoned. He's left to confront a monetary crisis and the remnants of a war. They built him up and let the world tear him apart as his own hubris blinded him to the facts of the situation.

"Left behind is an amateurish House of Representatives, whose silly minority conference appears not only out of sync with their presidential candidate, but with reality.

"Get a grip: You may get re-elected because no one had the sense to take you on, but you are as out of step as the Democrats you fought so hard to replace just 14 years ago.

"Then there's the Senate. Yes, senators were often prima donnas in my Senate staff years of the 1980s. (Fortunately, my boss wasn't one of them.) And Democrats then could be just as bad. A more imperious creature

than Sen. Robert Byrd of West Virginia was impossible to find back then.

"*Conservatives today are frustrated that America appears ready to elect an untested and liberal newcomer, Barack Obama; and to do it with issues still looming about his past political beliefs and associations.*

"*Voters aren't rejecting conservative values this year. All they know is that they can't stand the inarticulate, pompous bunch that now speaks for and represents the Republican and conservative causes.*

"*Although McCain has more experience in his little pinky than Obama does in his whole body, McCain likely never had a prayer this year.*

"*Most of this humdrum bunch of Republican elected officials never liked him much in the first place. Moreover, because of a basic inability to develop a message that would resonate with the public, McCain has been successfully portrayed as the third version of Bush.*

"*What will the Republican Party need to do if Nov. 4 turns into the sort of repudiation that puts comedians like Al Franken in the U.S. Senate and gives so-called 'red states' over to Obama?*

"*Clean house. Fresh, new candidates will have to find the courage to challenge Republican incumbents.*

"*Sarah Palin and others like her are the future of the GOP. It's Palin's humanity that energizes the party.*

"*Let the house of cards collapse. Then the GOP can rebuild its whole party.*

"*Nothing can be more fun or rewarding than having a cause greater than one's own personal political greed.*"

As for my other "feeling," well that was more like a frying pan hitting me upside the head. The combination of David Axelrod's transference of Chicago-style politics to the national arena, combined with the almost infallible cool and confident candidate Obama, was a force the likes of which I had never witnessed.

The Reagan Revolution also had been a tapping into America's frustrations, and Reagan had been every bit as cool and competent as Obama. But that particular brand of revolution had not been methodically planned out years in advance. In fact, it didn't really spring to life until the last month of the 1980 campaign.

Newt's 1994 takeover of Congress had been more methodically planned out than Reagan's ascent, but it never enjoyed the always cool and self-assured attitude put forth by Reagan. Nevertheless, to the credit of Gingrich and his Republican congressional leaders, they had been planning both with a message and with new campaign techniques. (Believe it or not, direct mail as a tool for persuading voters and raising money really didn't hit its stride until the 1980s. Essentially it was invented by conservative strategist and activist Richard Viguerie. Even prior to the 1980s, he had already pioneered a way to merge mass mailings on computer files.)

But Newt's revolution had to be planned on many fronts. It went back to the old days of the early 1980s, when strategists like Bob Weed, Joe Gaylord, and a legend in D.C. Republican politics, Wilma Goldstein, were holding court with younger protégés like me. We were testing ideas and searching for answers. But we didn't have a set playbook.

It seems odd now, but Gingrich wasn't sure that he and his buddies would take over the longtime Democratically controlled House until just a few days before the '94 election.

But nothing could compare to what I was witnessing from Barack Obama. Final campaign rallies would attract as many as 100,000 people. "Get Out the Vote" operations were perfected, with classes taught in swing states all over the nation by veterans of the civil rights movement, past democratic campaigns, and yes, community organizers. For a former political strategist and candidate, all of this was pure art.

In the final days of the campaign we were polling battleground states for Politico almost every day. We showed Obama ahead in Florida, Colorado, Pennsylvania, Virginia, and Ohio. Our polling indicated that even North Carolina, a Republican stronghold, was

a virtual tie. I had confidence in our weighting of the demographics and in the data we were collecting, using an advanced electronic
system that was lightening fast.

Unless I had missed my mark, the McCain campaign's strategy to attempt to take the normally Democratic state of Pennsylvania
away from Obama was a waste of the candidate's time and money.
If Virginia and Florida fell to Obama, there would be little hope for
McCain. And if he lost Ohio, there would be virtually none.

McCain's only real chance was to hold on to Florida and
Ohio and attempt to replicate other portions of the George W. Bush
2004 victory map. But with Colorado, which Bush had carried, looking like it was lost, and Nevada, another past Bush state going for
Obama, even that plan looked unlikely.

Halloween night, which fell on the Friday before the election, is a notoriously bad night for polling. Young parents are out with
their kids, young adults and some middle-agers are partying—it's a
real crap shoot. But with three-day running averages, one night's
worth of questionable numbers really would not reverse an obvious
trend. And the trend was obvious: Barack Obama, perhaps the most
unlikely of all of the major candidates to have been picked by the
pundits to win the White House in his maiden effort, was going to
become the next president of the United States. It was really all over
but the counting of the votes.

★ 38 ★

PARANOID VICTORY

I had the pleasure of appearing several times on Bill Maher's television show back when it was on ABC. Maher is often despised by conservatives, but those who actually know him—and they are many, and distinguished—he is a delight.

I couldn't help but laugh when I heard Bill talking to Larry King after the results of the presidential election had come in. He used the word "paranoid" as well. I knew once again I had chosen the right title!

Maher was using the word to explain how hard it was to believe that Barack Obama and the Democrats had actually won. In essence, he said that while the victory was obviously a fact, paranoia was so rampant that one expected Lucy (the cartoon character from Peanuts) to once again yank the football away just as Charlie Brown tried to kick it.

But there would be no snatching the football away from Obama. His crushing defeat of John McCain went beyond the best-hoped-for scenario for a Democratic candidate for president. Obama took away traditional "red" states from the GOP, including Ohio, Florida, Colorado, Nevada, and others now suddenly gone "blue."

I didn't devote a huge amount of this book to the background stories of McCain or Obama. Those have in many ways been written more than enough. Any genuinely new revelations might take years to come out. We'll leave that for the biographers.

But I did learn one late fact of interest. In best explains why a state like Iowa—typically Republican in presidential contests—fell so convincingly into Obama's column. Recall that Iowa's caucuses helped start the buzz that propelled Obama to the Democratic nomination.

The man in charge of Obama's national field operations might be called the ultimate "community organizer." It's obvious enough that he did one hell of a job. Much less known is that he began his earliest work within the first month of Obama entering as a freshman in the U.S. Senate, although that work was not officially on behalf of Obama for president. I was floored when I learned this. My unimpeachable source put it to me straight: "David Axelrod told Barack Obama before he was even sworn in as a senator that he would one day be the president of the United States."

In a sense, Axelrod was repeating history. It has long been known that John Kennedy's father made no secret of his intention to see his son become president, also about the time that John was entering the U.S. Senate (from a tenure in the U.S. House).

Axelrod specialized in what he called "urban politics," but he believed that same approach could be brought to main street America—in a national election. He was right.

Obama, having no father figure in his life, found Axelrod, who he met first in 1992. They bonded. Axelrod is known for being liberal and brilliant—nothing unusual for top Democratic strategists. But he is also known for being soft spoken, gentle, calm, and funny. Believe me, no matter which side of the political aisle you look on, that combination of attributes can rarely be found all in one political consultant.

In my estimation, Obama's other father figure was Larry Tribe. Tribe, writing for Forbes.com just one day after Obama's victory, entitled his piece, "Morning-After Pride." It was well deserved.

Tribe describes the feelings of pride he had for Obama as the two embraced at Obama's massive victory party in Chicago's Grant Park. Such moments, when years of friendship and years of hard work lead to such a phenomenal result, are truly rare, and when they occur the emotions they evoke are indescribable.

Tribe's eloquent article was a masterpiece of understatement, if anything. Nevertheless, a telling insight was his observation that Obama's election sealed, "a great divide in the biography of the United States. . . . As a nation we have come of age."

What Larry Tribe's morning-after commentary told me was that the dreams and hopes of those like Bob Shrum, Larry Tribe and their departed friend Jim Unger had come to fruition in a former law school research assistant's election to the presidency, and that that happening brought to life dreams that had died when Robert Kennedy was assassinated in 1968 and when Ted Kennedy failed to win his party's nomination in 1976.

The personal feelings were just as moving for those who had not known Obama. Once Ohio and Pennsylvania and Florida fell to Obama, it was obvious that America was making astounding history. My lifelong friend Tom Houck, who, as a young, white teenager was the personal driver for Dr. Martin Luther King, Jr., phoned me while I was stuck in a television studio. "I'm down here with everybody (from the civil rights years) . . . even Dexter and Marty and Bernice are all here together." The three remaining children of Dr. King had been sparring in court over whether their mother's letters should be released for a book, which Dexter had committed the family corporation to publishing. "I'm glad to hear they are all together," I said. "I wish you could be here," he said.

Now, you would ask, why would someone who was part of the early conservative Reagan revolution and who was Newt Gingrich's former chairman be welcome at such a gathering?

I was actually blessed to have grown up in the city that

Dr. King called home, Atlanta. I was equally blessed to have been born right when integration in the South was just beginning. That means memories of "whites only" water coolers and the like are just beyond my recall. .

In Atlanta some of the most conservative or Republican leaders have been the most supportive of the African-American community. Why? Because in the 1970s, 1980s, and even into the 1990s, Republicans and African Americans were both minorities, pretty much led around by white Democrats.

I've mentioned several nationally known talk show hosts who are often derided by liberals and most Democrats because of their conservative stands. But two of those hosts did the same thing that I did in the late 1980s and 1990s, by helping a "liberal" cause. Sean Hannity and Neal Boortz raised money and helped the late Rev. Hosea Williams—another of Dr. King's close aides in the civil rights movement—to feed thousands of hungry people every Thanksgiving and Christmas in Atlanta. Sean once jokingly said on the air that about four days before he was to help feed thousands of Atlanta's homeless, Hosea would call and say, "We're not going to make it."

I got the same call, as did Neal. None of us hesitated to write checks, attend news conferences, and go down to help Hosea with what he called "Feed the Hungry."

Atlanta is a rare city in America in that it would be impossible to have many friends or do much business if one weren't open to true friendship between races.

As a true Republican in my politically active days, I pushed for things like term limits and open records. And then there was one other thing, something that had unintended consequences and which, years later, I fought to reverse. In my syndicated column of March 1, 2007, I first tackled the growing national controversy over a young teenager named Genarlow Wilson. The headline was "Bad Legislation: A Real Nightmare."

"When I argued last week that Al Gore isn't necessarily out of the picture in the 2008 presidential race, I received many a note saying I was the only idiot writing such rubbish.

"If you watched the long and often boring Academy Awards last Sunday, you might have seen where I'm coming from. Newspaper headlines the next day declared, 'Gore Might Run.' James Carville penned a column saying Gore would run—and could win.

"But I definitely can be wrong. To illustrate, allow me to bring readers up to date on the real story behind the imprisonment of Genarlow Wilson, the young man who was in his teens when he was convicted of having sex with a minor and sentenced to 10 years. The case has made Georgia a source of national attention.

"It was a bad law that led to Wilson's 10-year mandatory sentence. What's worse, I was technically the author of the bill.

"At the time I introduced the 'Child Protection Act of 1995,' I was close with all political leaders in Georgia, was U.S. House Speaker Newt Gingrich's chairman, and had been named the National Republican Freshman Legislator of the Year several years earlier. So it wasn't hard for me to pass through the Georgia House, where I then served, a bill designed to punish truly heinous child molesters and others who abuse children.

"When the bill reached the state Senate, the chair of the Judiciary Committee insisted I add a Senate bill that would raise Georgia's outdated age of consent from fourteen to sixteen.

"There was just one problem: The committee chair refused to allow significant language that would have made it clear that with young people who engaged in sex, with one partner being below the age of consent, violators of the new law would not be subject to the portions of it that triggered a mandatory ten-year jail sentence.

"Being the cocky legislator I was, I fooled myself into believing that some vague language in the bill would prevent such a miscarriage of justice. Moreover, proponents of adding the age of consent portion to my bill--designed to punish truly bad people—argued that no prosecutor *would ever apply the ten-year provision to a case of two teenagers engaging in consensual sex. As an attorney who had successfully tried capital murder cases years previous, I thought I had enough legal experience to agree with them.*

"I passed the bill, and I've regretted it ever since. As soon as I realized the bill was being abused, I started writing about the error. I offered to provide any evidence, including statements by anyone willing, that it was not the intent of the author of the original bill to require young kids to serve ten years in jail.

"To make it clear on this specific case: Wilson, then seventeen, and his buddies made a videotape of Wilson having sex with a fifteen-year-old girl.

"But that matters little. The prosecutor sought a conviction for charges of rape, plus other aggravating charges. The jury found Wilson innocent of forcible rape and the other charges. He was convicted on a technicality of the bill I passed. A 10-year sentence, never intended, was imposed.

"In recent weeks I've spoken out in the media. Several of my former lawmaker colleagues have appeared to be hard and unsympathetic to the situation. But they too need to be given a break. They don't know the particulars of how the age-of-consent portion of the bill was forced onto my legislation. They have legitimate concerns about a current bill designed to address the issue. I believe the author of this current bill, and various other players of both political parties, will come together to pass a less drastic measure than the one now being offered—but one that nevertheless will clean up this mess and lead to Wilson's freedom.

"Let this be a lesson to young legislators. Think carefully before you pass legislation.

"And let this be a lesson, too, to those of us who have served in the past. It doesn't take courage to pass a law. It takes more to stand up and say when it's wrong.

"I only wish the other parties responsible for this situation would have joined former Lt. Gov. Pierre Howard and me in speaking out and

telling America the true story.''

Fortunately for Genarlow, he had a tenacious and fabulous lawyer, B.J. Bernstein, who took on his case and fought for his release. I joined B.J., offering my own *amicus* brief when the matter was under consideration by Georgia's Supreme Court.

Thankfully, Genarlow was set free.

Later, I learned that Andrew Young had nominated me and a courageous African American Georgia legislator, Emanuel Jones, for the John F. Kennedy Profile in Courage Award. I was shocked and honored. Andy's nomination was followed with an additional one. It came from Isaac Ferris, Dr. King's nephew and head of the King Center. In the letter, he nominated both Jones and me on behalf of the entire King family.

Needless to say, we didn't win the award. But I never expected to. Our award was the affirmation that, at least in the city I call home, we were way ahead of the curve with regard to race relations. I will admit that a few of my Republican friends in the state legislature were upset with me, but not for racially motivated reasons. They just felt strongly that Genarlow should stay in jail. I had, they argued, authored the bill and should have to live with it. But how, I asked, knowing that the interpretation was not my intent, could I live with myself?

Thankfully, the Georgia Supreme Court relieved me of that burden.

So yes, I could understand the euphoria that my friends who had labored in the civil rights movement for decades were enjoying. If you weren't moved by the historic moment of Barack Obama's win—even if you opposed him based on issues and philosophy—you probably needed to reassess where your soul was and where it needed to be.

★ 39 ★

FAREWELL TO THE MAVERICK

McCain really never had a prayer of winning the 2008 presidential race. The Republican establishment despised McCain for his willingness to cross the aisle to work with Democrats, and his equal willingness to cross the system by taking on George W. Bush in the 2000 election. He wasn't their kind of conservative. So they preferred to let him wilt on the vine, struggling for money, searching for issues, and having to deal with a leaky, creepy, Bush-linked staff, who decided that it was far more important to attack Sarah Palin before the election was even over than to really to win.

And McCain wouldn't get down into the gutter. He could have run endless Jeremiah Wright ads toward the end of the campaign. But McCain was bright enough to know that it would only have destroyed his own reputation, and not given him enough votes to overcome the inevitable tide of Obama votes. Although to me Wright seemed a fair topic, along with numerous other issues related to Sen. Obama's past—the time for raising his name again had passed.

You see, it was never supposed to be, a McCain race, that is. Mitt Romney—who I will freely admit I had warmed up to considerably by the end of the campaign—was meant to be the inheritor of the GOP establishment crowd. If not, they would settle for Rudy Giuliani. But when Mike Huckabee stole the show in the November 2007

CNN debate, he became the darling of populist and social conservatives long enough to deflate Romney and Giuliani to also-rans.

Ironically, the media in America, particularly the national press, have always liked McCain. They knew he would buck the system, was accessible, quotable and, open to them. It wasn't until he won his party's nomination that they attacked his every move.

But in the end, it was neither his choice of Sarah Palin nor his performances in the debates—not even his Joe the Plumber strategy—that did John McCain in. Instead it was an economic collapse rooted in a rotten housing market, propped up by a phony mortgage market, that for some reason decided to collapse and bring down with it the entire U.S. economy with just weeks to go before the election.

McCain was guilty of doing what he had taken a solemn oath to do: deal with the situation. Obama handled the crisis in the same manner. But McCain's party, fractured and broken, could not decide whether to trust a badly damaged President Bush who warned Congress of almost dire immediate consequences if a so-called "bailout bill" was not passed immediately or the phone calls from constituents, the very same who had put Bush back in office in 2004 by a huge margin. They demanded that Congress reject any bailout.

McCain was trapped between what he believed would put his country or his campaign first. As had been his tradition, he opted for, whether one agrees or not, country first. His fate was sealed.

Ironically, only a day after the election ended, pundits and writers from many national news organizations were musing that they "really didn't know much about Barack Obama." They were right.

So America entered a new era of change, not knowing if Obama would become the next John Kennedy if he would meet the comparisons immediately drawn or those earlier in the year to Jimmy Carter. Thankfully he had survived the campaign season without being harmed, a constant fear justified when a group of white supremacists was arrested just days before the election for having plotted Obama's assassination.

We would have none of that. Instead we needed, as we came to the end of the 2008 race, to pray for the safety and success of our president, be he Republican or Democrat—liberal or conservative.

And we needed to thank John McCain, a man who suffered physically for his country as a soldier and battled valiantly and honorably for his party, even if they never wanted him in the first place.

Ironically in the closing days of the race, I heard Mitt Romney on talk shows across America. Sarah Palin, when asked if she was interested in running for president in 2012 said, "No." But then again, she noted that she was responding after a grueling campaign.

Everyone involved in the 2008 campaign exited the stage with an army of followers. Palin returned to Alaska with her staff and Secret Service protection. President-elect Obama plunged into the duties of facing a deeply troubled economy surrounded by staff and advisors. Joe Biden was now surrounded by more security and plenty of staff.

As for me, after being on the air and giving interviews for a solid 24 hours, I entered my home the day after the election. My wife handed me a special overnight package. It was from Newt Gingrich, outlining the achievements of his Americans Solutions group in 2008.

I gently placed it on my desk in a stack labeled: to be read before 2012. I knew what it meant.

As for John McCain, unlike other politicians with their cadre of aides and security details, he drove his own car back to his Sedona ranch, accompanied by just one person—his friend Lindsey Graham. I jokingly noted that the GOP, known for always "eating its young," had now managed to eat "its old" too!

And as for Barack Obama, the stock market suffered its biggest loss since the crash of 1987 in the two days following his election. It was clear that change was needed, but what kind of change remained to be determined. It would be the first test for a man who seemed more than confident that he could rely on the "best and brightest" for assistance, but that title has already been used. So, as the end of the Bush years came into focus and the start of the Obama presidency began, it was fair to say that America remained a bit on edge, a bit unsure, a bit the same paranoid nation that started this whole thing to begin with. It remained to be seen where the nation would be four years later.

★ **ACKNOWLEGMENTS** ★

There are far too many people to thank—not just for their help with this book—but also for having helped provide me the opportunity to be the "Forrest Gump" of American politics— than I have space on these pages to acknowledge. So, let me simply thank a few people who played a critical role with this particular book.

First, thanks to my wife, children (now grown), and parents for putting up with my career, or better yet, many careers.

Second, thanks to my past and my current colleagues at InsiderAdvantage/Poll Position. They are among the nation's most respected pollsters and journalists and I deeply appreciate their devotion and assistance.

Critical to the production of this book was the publisher and the editors at Hill Street Press; my longtime friend in publishing Scott Bard; my great friend and associate Tom Houck; and Gary Reese, the most talented writer I have ever known, who helped step in and polish my work, as he always does.

My longtime co-worker and assistant Tricia Ruggiero was invaluable in getting this project actually completed.

And thanks to my friend C.B. Hackworth for encouraging me to write a book about the 2008 presidential race.

I've learned that the less lengthy the acknowledgments, the better the book. I don't know if that will prove to be the case, but regardless I'll stop while I'm ahead.

Oh, and one last thing: every story I personally recount in this book is absolutely true . . . and just think of the stories I didn't tell!